Education and Psychology of the Gifted Series

JAMES H. BORLAND, Editor

Nurturing Talent
in High School

Life in the Fast Lane

LAURENCE J. COLEMAN

Foreword by Joyce VanTassel-Baska

Teachers College, Columbia University
New York and London

Published by Teachers College Press, 1234 Amsterdam Avenue, New York, NY 10027

Library of Congress Cataloging-in-Publication Data

Coleman, Laurence J.
    Nurturing talent in high school : life in the fast lane / Laurence J. Coleman.
        p. cm. — (Education and psychology of the gifted series)
    Includes bibliographical references and index.
    ISBN 0-8077-4612-6 (cloth : alk. paper)
    1. Gifted children—Education (Secondary)—United States—Research. 2. Gifted children—United States—Conduct of life. 3. Gifted children—United States—Attitudes. I. Title. II. Series.
    LC3993.23.C65   2005
    371 96'73—dc22   2005044045

ISBN 0-8077-4612-6 (cloth)

Printed on acid-free paper
Manufactured in the United States of America

12   11   10   09   08   07   06   05   8   7   6   5   4   3   2   1

Contents

Foreword

Larry Coleman's book *Nurturing Talent in High School: Life in the Fast Lane* is a delightful qualitative study, conducted by a master, on an important archetypical program context in gifted education—the residential high school. He depicts the lives of selected students in a series of case studies, but also goes well beyond this by attempting to establish a grounded theory of life in these residential "hot houses." The book represents a landmark study of our field in many ways. It effectively documents the issues that inhabitants of such schools face. It also examines the program characteristics that facilitate the talent development of these young people, even as these features contribute to greater stress and pressure for student life in the Greenhouse Institute—from the routines of dormitory living to the weekend spontaneity of all night sessions and pranks. In eight chapters, Dr. Coleman provides a rich look at students' lives, their families, and the place that binds them together during the latter years of high school.

The book is also a tribute to a small segment of American society that defies the stereotype of "the lazy American student who goes for the easy grade." Rather than seeing high school as a social playground and sports camp, it depicts highly gifted learners as earnest in their quest for intellectual challenge and rigor, and their families as hard working, caring, and persistent in providing support.

Coleman's central premise is that the Greenhouse Institute has a unique social system characterized by the opening and closing forces that permeate it. These forces are characterized as the constant interaction of students and families with program characteristics to produce a learning community around the shared values of excellence and diversity, the understanding of impermanence and fluidity in the learning situation, the stress that comes with new challenges and opportunities, the pervasive sense of belonging as a tactic secret of how the institution works, and the need for information flow at all levels of the enterprise. This grounded theory of what makes the Greenhouse Institute unique is a major contribution to our understanding of the power of residential high schools.

Coleman uses interesting metaphors throughout the text to capture difficult ideas and concepts. The "greenhouse" metaphor is suggestive of both the structural care and attention these students receive in order to ensure that their talent "blooms," and also the closed constraints imposed on their lives under the optimal conditions provided. The metaphor of a "soloist musician" is employed in the case studies to help explain individual differences within the common themes of the institution to illustrate how different students react to situations within the environment. They therefore "interpret" these situations in unique ways that "play out" for them within their learning style, subject matter preferences, and social networks.

Coleman suggests that, as human beings test their limits in a relatively safe environment, they encounter more of their own humanity. This idea is an interesting one. It suggests the need for individuals to strive in order to appreciate their own and others' capacities. It represents an ode to effortful education in this country, an approach long embraced by other cultures but often mocked by our own. Yet his portrait of the residential high school embodies the equal emphasis on ability and effort in meaningful academic achievement. Would that such a model represented the new direction for all of secondary education in this country!

Coleman's treatment of the effects of poverty and being undereducated in a high-powered setting like the Greenhouse Institute is highly effective. A sight that disturbed him greatly was seeing talented students brought low by the misperception that they lack ability, rather than viewing the situation as involving a lack of educational opportunity. The truth for such students in these settings is that they will under-perform, based on years of neglect in critical areas of learning for which ability alone cannot rescue them. Caring teachers who work in tutorials with such learners and perceptive counselors who address issues of self worth are the best antidotes to the problem once it surfaces. Coleman also believes that the intrinsic motivation of such students to succeed in a challenging environment can contribute strongly to their ultimate success. Such inner drive and determination was on display often in the Greenhouse Institute. However, the best long-term solutions to "educational malnourishment" rest in equalizing educational opportunities for gifted learners throughout the country and providing appropriate experiences early, regardless of type of school district or geographical location.

Another interesting idea Coleman tackles is the perception of academic talent development as undesirable because of its very real difference from the process of creating well-rounded individuals. Talent development requires years of practice and learning the skill of a domain, attention to creativity-relevant tools/skills, and strong motivation to work in a particular field, fueled by a passion and commitment to it. This is not an algorithm for well-roundedness, and consequently suggests that the academic residential high school is in the business of breeding future scientists, mathematicians, and economists, not politicians. This idea of early field-based specialization is one that many Americans may find disturbing, yet for talent development to flourish in this country there have to be contexts that allow rapid and advanced development in specific areas of ability in order to hasten the onset of creative productivity in several fields. Not all gifted students need to fit the niche of "well-rounded" in order to contribute importantly to their society, an understanding worth noting in light of Coleman's book. We are producing the next generation of creators in these schools, a significant enough enterprise in its own right.

Dangers for such institutions abound, however, according to Coleman. Should the residential high school ever be perceived as the only route to "success" in this country, the proliferation of replications could become problematic as both the curriculum and the balancing of relationships would occur in ways that might compromise both excellence and diversity. His sense of the need to maintain the "optimal match" between learners and curriculum challenge is admirable, given our propensity as a society to offer the same diet to all learners, regardless of their readiness to partake.

There is also always present the danger of parochialism and self-satisfaction, where faculty and staff become too comfortable in their situation and stop growing. These schools, as Coleman rightly points out, are compromises between high school and colleges. While demanding in some respects, they do not require the management skills of a typical high school nor the productivity expectations for publication of most colleges. Therefore, they are a perfect context for many bright teachers seeking a comfort zone in their career. Unfortunately, once such a facility becomes entrenched, it is difficult to motivate teachers to embrace new ideas, to test new pedagogy, and to rise to higher levels of performance. In the absence of an attitude of self-improvement, such schools can easily become stagnant and lose the dynamism Coleman so admires.

This book is also a primer for qualitative researchers interested in trying to use these techniques in their own research efforts. Coleman not only explicitly identifies the standard process that he employs to carry out the work, carefully stating research bias, striving for credibility through member checking and the use of multiple sources, and using thick description filtered through the researcher's diary to assess subjectivity and reflexivity. He also brings his readers along on the journey by sharing his doubts, his concerns, and those nagging issues about decisions he has made in managing and interpreting the data. I found particularly interesting his grappling with decisions over which case studies to highlight in the book. His sensitivity to the need for representativeness is always tempered by the insistent emergent themes that ultimately hold sway in his decision-making. Laying bare these moments of uncertainty in data management and interpretation may also prove instructional, as well as encouraging, to novices attempting this type of research.

Nurturing Talent in High School: Life in the Fast Lane is a must-read for all researchers and practitioners in the field of gifted education as it blends an important methodological approach with a topic of great interest. The insights produced warrant a closer look at current theory, research, and practice in the field with an eye toward greater appreciation of the rigors, ambiguities, and triumphs of the academic talent development process in individual lives and families.

—Joyce VanTassel-Baska

Acknowledgments

Nurturing Talent in High School: Life in the Fast Lane took 1 year in the field and 4 years at my desk. I could not have accomplished this project without the help and encouragement of the people mentioned below. The logistical resources they provided were necessary, but their emotional support was even more critical.

Richard Wisniewski became the dean of the College of Education, University of Tennessee, and brought his interest in qualitative research. He provided faculty who had a faint interest in the opportunity to explore the genre. I discovered a habit of mind that enabled me to pursue my research interests in a manner that was more consistent with my worldview than the path I had been on. Without that nudge, I am not sure I would ever have taken the step that changed my scholarly career and eventually led to this undertaking.

Betty Ann Daggett Coleman, my partner of many years, has supported, and sometimes endured, my professional and political passions. Besides joining with me to raise three daughters, she pursued her own professional and political agenda and still found time to provide feedback on many of my writing projects. I am a lucky man.

Tracy Cross saw the potential value of this study and helped find the financial resources necessary to do it. Throughout the study he did not waiver in our agreement to never ask evaluative questions. I admire his honor and welcome his friendship.

The faculty and students of the Greenhouse Institute let me into their world and into their lives. Without the students' willingness to share their thoughts and activities while we lived the GI experience together, I would have told a different story. I am especially beholden to my eight prime participants. They gave up many hours in tight schedules to talk with me. I am grateful to the Teaching Fellows of the Greenhouse Institute who were inspirational in their willingness to suspend their successful lives as public school teachers in order to keep learning about children and teaching. Sharing their beginners' eyes was most validating.

My original colleagues (Amos Hatch, Kermit Blank, Susan Benner, Lynn Cagle) in the Inclusive Early Childhood program at the University of Tennessee, Knoxville, whose commitment to reforming teacher education and willingness to engage in collaborative scholarship enabled me to keep alive interests in gifted education, teacher education, and qualitative research. I was fortunate to have been able to live in an open, supportive, collaborative academic community with them.

The qualitative research support groups at the University of Tennessee, where I began this study, and at the University of Toledo, where I finished writing it, provided constructive criticism along the way.

Lastly, I want to thank people who have played a lesser but important role in this project. They are: Tracy Delphia, who came to my rescue as a transcriber and provided interesting, unsolicited comments on the data; Lilla Horton, who helped with the final stages of the manuscript; Charlie Dabbs and Tom Hebert, who read the initial draft, bringing a fresh perspective; and Judy Daso Herb, who, by providing the resources for my present academic position, enabled me to finish this book with much less torment than previous writing projects.

CHAPTER ONE

Entering the Fast Lane

Fourteen-year-olds who regard themselves as serious about learning and want more academics do not represent the typical portrait of the American adolescent as portrayed in the media. Teenagers who want to develop their academic talents and are willing to leave their local high school and home to fulfill that desire are considered to be out of the ordinary. Yet such teenagers exist, and there are schools where they can go, without needing to be rich. In this story, one state among the 50 decided to nourish academic talent by selecting children and placing them in a special residential program.

The Greenhouse Institute (GI), a fictitious name, is a 2-year residential high school designed to develop nascent academic talent in adolescents. This book seeks to understand the students who go there, what the Greenhouse Institute is like for them, how they live there, and the community that is established by the interplay between students and the Institute. GI creates conditions that produce a multicultural community that honors diversity and excellence, an outcome not found in typical high schools. Throughout the book, I seek to offer an explanation for how the school and the students sustain an atypical, open learning community.

Readers looking for a story of best educational practices will not find it here. Information can be found about education practice, but I make few evaluations of the school. Rather, this is a story of one special school with its own characteristics and practices that make sense within that setting. I cannot say things should be the same in other places as they were at GI.

I settled on the name "Greenhouse Institute" because it denotes two aspects of the place, one metaphoric and one concrete. Metaphorically, GI reminded me of a hothouse where young plants are rushed to maturity. Concretely, GI is an organization bound by constraints of time, culture, and politics that set the context for the story of the students who chose to attend the special program. The students' stories cannot be understood without an appreciation of the institution. The subtitle, *Life in the Fast Lane*, highlights the students' intention to enter an educational environment that amplified their own tendencies for rapid development and for serious learning.

The purpose of the study is to describe the lives of students in a special public 2-year residential high school using their own voices. It is significant to learn about life in this high school because it is a specialized environment where potential talent meets opportunity. In over 2 decades of study I have come up with two propositions about gifted children: (1) children finding themselves in a generally hostile culture adapt to that reality, and (2) the emergence of a talent is not a consequence of lone individuals triumphing over adversity, but rather one of people who find themselves, consciously or unconsciously, to be in environments that facilitate their growth (Coleman, 1997). In other words, the development of talent is a cultural and personal phenomenon. This ethnographic study happens in an educational setting where young people possessing signs of a rudimentary talent have chosen to attend in order to be educated by people who want them to reach their potential.

Ethnography enables one to study the common interactions of a culture. I am interested in the ordinary rather than the extraordinary interactions that influence talent development in settings because most growth occurs off center stage, away from the exultant moments. Talent development takes place in situations where joy may be present, where frustration is a common emotion, and where deliberate practice is the behavior most evident. I hoped this study would give me insight into what happens in a single setting to one group of children with potential for advanced development so that I might be able to share those insights with colleagues who study the development of talent and with the talented children and their families.

Capturing the life of the students in the school is important because no source is presently available that describes the life in such schools. Significantly, I have learned enough from audiences composed of people who work, teach, or have gone to schools like this in our country or abroad that my description of the school has a universal quality that extends beyond this particular setting. Another valuable reason for depicting life in the Greenhouse Institute is to provide descriptions to students and their families in a manner that enables them to make more informed decisions about whether to become involved in such a school. Less than a dozen public residential high schools exist in this country. Deciding to leave home and go to a special school is not a trivial decision for these families.

Understanding and interpreting the experience of talent development is my other reason for doing this ethnography. I anticipated discovering much about how children make sense of their own development and what adults think they are doing to encourage that development in a special setting. My intention was to interpret the student perspective in the form of an explanatory theory.

Many gifted children feel pressure to deny interests and to resist their propensity for rapid learning in typical educational settings (Coleman & Cross, 1988). What would I find in a place that is supposed to be an inviting, growth-oriented kind of environment? What pressures would be an issue in GI? The idea that environment makes a difference is significant because advanced development is fostered in special settings, such as think tanks, Olympic sports camps, clubs, special music schools, Talent Search Programs, and so forth (Bloom, 1985). We do not know how participants, especially young people, experience those settings and how a setting works for or against the development it intends to promote. Obviously, students will learn lots of information and academic skills, but what else might they learn? Will I find that the nonacademic learning in a special setting like GI is important? Do the social system and values that operate in a place like GI parallel the usual high school experience? Can I construct a grounded theory of life at GI?

HOW I GOT INVOLVED IN THE GREENHOUSE INSTITUTE

My arrival at the Greenhouse Institute was not an accident. I have been an advocate for the education of gifted and talented children for 20 years. As part of that role, I was a cofounder of the Tennessee Association for the Gifted. Not only have I been an advocate of legislation, but I have also been a founder of two educational programs for children: the University Summer Enrichment Program and the Summer Institute for Gifted Children. The former no longer exists; the latter is now being run by some of the original students. In addition to being an advocate, I have also had other roles—namely, as teacher, counselor, professor, and editor of a scholarly journal, *The Journal for the Education of the Gifted*, sponsored by the Association for the Gifted of the Council for Exceptional Children.

Observing children in those programs crystallized my interest in the experience of being gifted from the student's perspective. Listening in the night after the lights went out in a camp dormitory, the quiet talk was filled with references to school experiences. Many comments were expressions of dismay and discomfort with the contradictory and inhospitable circumstances of schools. One conversation I recall decades later was of one boy explaining the problem of maintaining attention as a class reviewed work he understood, having his mind wander to more interesting subjects, recalling the teacher's ridicule and wondering aloud why this happened, since the teacher knew he understood the subject that was being taught. Those overheard conversations, doubts about the conventional wisdom that the source of underachievement in gifted children was emotional problems, and other experiences as a teacher impelled me to conduct research on the experience of being gifted.

My interest in gifted children and their education has been the center-piece of my professional career. In the last dozen years I have become interested in interpretive inquiry, a more qualitative orientation, as a way to understand teaching and giftedness. The change in methodology and an ongoing reflection on my meta-theoretical orientation to research has led me to question the way in which we study the development of giftedness and talents. I became intrigued by David Feldman's work (1994) on nonuniversal development and by Lev Vygotsky's (1978, 1987) work on social settings and zones of proximal development. These influences have contributed to a growing belief that research on the development of giftedness could profit by a shift from a focus on the individual to the study of settings in which individuals develop. Because most examples of giftedness in adults are essentially instances of nonuniversal development and that examples of advanced development could be traced to being in social settings in which children were stretched (zones of proximal) to develop their talent, I reasoned that research into programs in which people with potential talents are grouped would be an advantageous place to study the development of giftedness (Coleman, 1995, 1997).

LIVING THE STUDENTS' EXPERIENCE

Once I got the invitation to the Greenhouse Institute, I was mindful that the parameters of my relationship with people in the school and with the administration had to be established. My purpose was to gather information on the student experience, not to engage in any evaluation of staff or program. While the director refrained assiduously from asking evaluative comments, almost everyone else (administrators, residence counselors, staff, teachers, and students) asked, What do you think about this particular practice or that kid or these rules? In those instances I deflected their questions by repeating that I was there to learn what it was like to be a student. My neutral position was constant. When I expressed an opinion, I gave neutral descriptions. I became adept at reversing the question so that the person who asked supplied the answer.

I became part of the place. Returning in January after a holiday, students and faculty commented, "We missed you," and "Where were you?" Late in the spring, my self-congratulatory sense of fitting in was shaken when a student asked, "Who are you?" and "What are you doing here?"

I knew before I arrived that the school had two big divisions: academic life and residential life. Spending time in both domains was pivotal for understanding student life. I wanted to do everything the students did. However, there were some real constraints due to age, gender, and purpose for being at the school. I am a tall man in his 50s with an almost white beard. Passing for a teenager with a typical relationship with a roommate would never work. So I did not have one. I wanted to live on the girls' side of the dorm to sample their life, too, but my presence in the girls' dorm would not have been acceptable to parents, even though I have lived with four women in my own home.

However, my room was physically the same as any boys' room, including poor heating and cooling systems. I lived by the same dorm schedule as the students did. My credibility with the students grew with the realization that I used the community bathrooms, ate the same food, and followed the same rules. I was told, "You are the only one who knows. No adult has done it." The meanings in the statement are important on many levels.

I dressed in a manner to make me acceptable to the faculty and staff as well as to the students. The students, of course, looked like typical teenagers in oversized clothes, backpacks, sweatshirts, and athletic-looking shoes. I, too, carried a backpack loaded with notebooks, disks, and a tape recorder. I openly carried a notebook everywhere, even to dinner at a restaurant with adults.

Living like a student did not mean that I resided in the dorm the entire time I was at the Greenhouse Institute. The school had arranged for me to live in a university-owned apartment complex when I was not living in the dorm. The primary reason was to allow me to coordinate life at GI with my responsibilities in Knoxville. Furthermore, I discovered that I needed time to speak with adults alone and that did not fit into the dorm schedule. Living in the dorm 24 hours a day also made it almost impossible to keep up with my field notes. So a refuge was most welcome. An unanticipated benefit, my apartment was in a complex where the teaching fellows—high school teachers who come to GI for a year—were staying. This proximity created an opportunity for friendship with other "outsiders" in the GI community who provided another look into the school and its students.

I did not live like a student in another way. Students have only their dorm room. I needed space so I could talk privately with people who had no access to my dorm room. I shared a space with a computer server that opened onto a major corridor used by both adults and students. This was another serendipitous location because it allowed for opportunities for people to drop in and chat—another rich source of data.

Collecting Rich Data

Gathering data and writing field notes became addictive. During the first month almost every experience or thought I could recall was written into my field notes. I made entries in a 6 x 9-inch spiral notebook from the moment

I awoke until I went to sleep. A new notebook was used each month. The August notebook was full; the April and May notebook was comparatively empty. These notes included names of people and descriptions of them, maps of various settings, conversations, and reflections or notes to me. Upon returning to my apartment or my dorm room, I would expand my notes while entering them into a computer. I worked until I fell asleep.

By the end of the first month, as I prepared to leave for a week, I was struggling to keep up. Driving alone to Knoxville and back to GI, I recognized that I had to change from the industrial vacuum cleaner approach of data collection to a more deliberate approach that sought specific information. I decided to limit my time in the field to 8 hours a day. Eventually, it averaged somewhere around 6 and 8 hours, excepting the 24 hour days when I lived in the dorm.

My basic fieldwork strategy was to "go with the flow" of the place and not draw attention to myself. I simply showed up at events. I asked teachers permission to be in their classrooms. I wanted them to accept the fact that I was studying the students and not them. My persistent burning questions were as follows: What are the students doing? Where are they if I cannot see them? What am I overlooking? By the end of September, I knew the pace, location, vocabulary, smells, and sounds of the place so "disturbances in the force" caught my attention and were entered in my field notes. I capitalized on serendipitous events, which proved to be important sources of data. When opportunities presented themselves, I joined in. For example, I joined a "run," which is when a residence counselor takes students off campus for some reason, usually to get food. Tagging along enabled me to see and talk with students away from the patterned environment of classes and the dorm and to build special connections with them.

"Hanging around" was an effective means to discover patterns. I departed from the general approach by inventing techniques to get more focused data. I wanted to understand what students were doing when they left the GI complex, how they regarded such actions, and what affect leaving had on their experience. I hung around the lounge and sign-out desk, speaking with students. I would walk with them as they went out, if I was invited. I went places I thought they would show up, such as stores, restaurants, and playgrounds, and observed them if and when they did.

Another category of behavior I wanted to understand was rule-breaking. How and when did this happen? How did kids think about it? I particularly wanted to know how much "illegal" smoking occurred, where was it happening, and when. I observed smokers who left the building, at what times, and with whom. By correlating that, I could discern patterns of smoking and associated behaviors by watching and listening.

The dining hall was one place where lots of information could be gleaned by eavesdropping or joining various tables. In the beginning I waited to be invited to join the students; after a while, I simply joined a group like everyone else. Becoming simply the ever-present person resulted in me hearing one boy sharing with another a story of attempting to crash a college party (a GI prohibition), and hearing "He is alright," meaning I would not tell the authorities. In general, the process of watching and listening revealed friendships, romances, and so forth.

Shadowing a student for a day, or shorter period of time, was a great way to get information. While with a student who was walking to class or eating breakfast, I would ask, "Do you mind if I follow you around for the day so I can learn more about how students spend their time?" That approach got me entry into situations where the conversations were chiefly among students, not between kids and adults. I attended announced meetings of various clubs, disciplinary meetings, student government sessions, counselor-called dorm meetings, performances, and sports events in order to see what typically happened. At one point I was invited by a student to join a club so they would have enough participants to call themselves a club.

Moving from collecting every piece of data to collecting data that would help complete the story of life at GI is a continual process of refocusing. That process of focusing was influenced by several factors, such as likability of people, doubts about the credibility of my data, people dropping in to talk, and so forth. Sometimes, focusing came from the realization that I was not actually doing what I intended. Reviewing field notes one weekend, I noted that many entries for that week were about conversations with adults and not about students. Focusing most often occurred when a question arose in the data. Several modifications in interviewing came from the need for more data. In one instance, I conducted a focus interview with seven senior girls because I thought my data on that group was weak; in another, I asked my eight prime participants to invite another person of their choice to one interview because I wondered whether they would speak differently in the presence of another and who they would bring. In these ways I examined friendship patterns and received unexpected insight into boy-girl relationships.

"Dropping in to talk" by students and faculty in the office space that I shared with a computer server or in my dorm room provided rich data about the intensity of the experience, the concept of home, the perceptions of faculty and residential counselors, school politics, and much more. These unplanned opportunities pointed to new areas of focus and were a useful way to triangulate information and sources. Some of my most memorable conversations happened this way. The conversations usually started with a question to me that morphed into a story about themselves and the school. After those conversations concluded, I fiendishly made entries into my field notes as soon as possible.

The most important source of focusing came directly from the students themselves. I would ask casually, What should I know to understand what it is like being a student here? A self-selected group of boys and girls produced a list of "things you should do if you really want to know what it is like." Examples were washing clothes, using the university library, eating the food, staying up late, and doing an all-nighter. I made certain to do everything listed.

Maximize Time to Write and Analyze

I lost this intention early in the process and never reached a point when I was satisfied that I was using time wisely for analysis and writing. I was excited that I was gathering ethnographic data on a phenomenon that my field had not studied. Every new experience caught my attention and fired my imagination. I created computer files for a "diary," for "my subjectivity" and for "reflexivity." My fear of missing something important that would ruin the study pushed me to feverishly collect data. In this conflicted state, I was consumed by doing field notes, sleeping, and eating.

In retrospect, I let the excitement of the data collection and my own insecurity about missing significant data thrust me toward bad practice. Not having proper time to rework field notes or time to think weakens the power of field notes. One change I implemented was to write less completely in my notebook and then expand my field notes more directly into the computer. This left more time to write. I never used my time to write wisely. The search for rich data trumped my analytical writing. In essence, I did minimal analytic writing while in the field, other than keeping up with my field notes, collecting documents, and making plans to do more of the same.

Scheduling Interviews That Sample the Kids

The fall semester provided me with a wealth of information. I built a network of participants whom I saw regularly. Eighty-nine student names appear in my field notes. The diversity among the students was obvious. I wanted to interview members of all groups, assuming they had varying perspectives on life at the school. In my mind I "split" the student body across these dimensions: sex, race, year at GI (such as junior, senior), ethnicity, academic orientation (science, humanities, etc.), geographic home (urban, rural, etc.), socioeconomic status, sexual orientation, membership in clubs, membership on teams, country of origin, and my familiarity with them.

I agonized for 2 months making list after list of "best" interviewees. At one time I had 32 people I planned to interview monthly in an elaborate scheme in the spring semester. I fought accepting that I could not possibly interview all the combinations, given the time constraints. In the end my list of splits became a guide for selecting students with whom I had a relationship and believed would make good informants. I tempered my selection by trying for an even number by sex and by school class. I also wanted the three biggest racial groups represented (white, black, Asian) and some geographical representation. Once I filled a category, I would not ask another. For example, when a junior from a rural school happened by and accepted, I would not ask another rural person to be an interviewee, even if such a person appeared. So, in this opportunistic way my participants were chosen. In the final group of eight, I had one student who was part Native American, a student who was a first-generation Asian American, a child of divorce, a low-income urban student, a student from a farm family, and a suburban middle-class student. I believe I got a reasonable cross section of the Greenhouse Institute's population. I am unsure of their representativeness of the student body at large, but the redundancy among their transcripts encapsulated much of the culture of the school.

Composing My Interviews

Throughout my stay, I had composed a list of questions for a semistructured interview guide and piloted it before the first interview. My first round of interviews used general questions. For example, two questions were: (1) I have heard students describe themselves as a math person or a science person. In what category would you put yourself? Tell me more about what that means to you; and (2) Starting with Sunday at bedtime, take me through your schedule for the next 2 days. The interview lasted about 70 minutes. I typically started with the same opening question and then went in the direction that seemed best for that interview. When questions were not covered, I moved them to the next interview. On my trips to Knoxville and back I listened to the tapes in my car and made notes at rest stops. I used tape recordings of the interviews to redesign the next interview. Thus, continuity was created that enabled me to check consistency of themes across interviews. One person did the final transcriptions and I listened again and again as I edited them.

DISCOVERING WHAT IS IN THE DATA

Discovering what is in the data is a process of gathering, defining, and discarding. I consistently kept a diary of reflections on the process as well as a list of potential themes. The major themes I stress in the book were present in the beginning, but took time to become figural in my thinking. My early categories were the contextual features of the Greenhouse Institute that anyone could readily see—such as dorm life, life in classrooms, administrative philosophy and mission, students, physical place, and so forth. These labels begin to cluster into groups such as daily schedule, math classes, homework, and power. On my trips home I reworked the list by questioning myself about my definitions for the terms. I became more and more focused and began to look at things, such as kinds of homework, friendships, resistance, rules, and the social system.

It was not until I left the field that I had time for deeper analysis and synthesis. I experienced the larger categories and subcategories remaining in my thoughts, while they became the backdrop for seeing deeper patterns of meaningful interactions. Over the summer and early fall, I created themes that integrated the old and newer categories, such as who owns the kids, rule bending, the rhythm of the schedule, and paradoxical learning. When I returned for a member check with the students and adults at GI 4 months later, my analysis was greeted with acceptance.

SUMMARY OF THE CONTENTS OF THIS BOOK

This book contains less of the Greenhouse Institute story than I could tell. My final decision to keep in or exclude data was based on two tenets of grounded theory: the story must be told in terms that participants would readily understand and the narrative has to be accessible so it can be used by participants with varying backgrounds (Glazer & Strauss, 1967) and later work (Strauss & Corbin, 1990).

Nurturing Talent in High School is an ethnography that interprets the student perspective of living 1 year in a special residential high school. The study and students' lives are examined over eight chapters. The book begins by describing the Greenhouse Institute in general and how I entered that environment. Specifics of life in the fast lane emerge in Chapter 2, where we learn how students apply to the school; what they encounter physically, socially, and academically when they arrive; and the tacit elements in the GI culture that influence the students' experiences. Chapter 3 takes us into the heart of GI by revealing the major themes of life in the fast lane. The two dominant organizational divisions of the school, Academic Life and Residential Life, are explored in detail in the next two chapters. In Chapter 4, I look at the academic demands of GI and how this changes the students' conception of and attitudes toward high school. Chapter 5 covers the Residential Life program. I explore how the Greenhouse Institute becomes a home for students. Chapter 6 looks deeper into the students' experience of living and learning in the fast lane by examining emergent issues such as academic resistance, educational malnourishment, and the value of curriculum. Chapter 7 offers an explanation of how the Greenhouse Institute produces a high school culture that honors excellence and diversity by proposing a grounded theory of life in the fast lane. Chapter 8 discusses the metaphors I used to understand the student experience and explores issues surrounding a school like GI. The book ends with an epilogue that answers questions about how one can do ethnography and have a full professional and personal life.

MY INFLUENCE ON THE FINDINGS

My intent is to tell the students' stories from their perspective, but the simple fact is that it is *my* take on *their* perspective. In interpretive scholarship all data are filtered through the researcher's mind. Understanding who has conducted the research determines much of the credibility and trustworthiness of the findings (Denzin & Lincoln, 1994). Throughout the book, I provide information relevant to the issues of trustworthiness and credibility, such as evidence of prolonged engagement, thick description, and member checking. I report only themes that are supported by multiple sources (students, documents, and adults) and multiple methods (participant observation, documents, and interviews), that have been shared with the participants in person or by e-mail, and that have been given for critique to colleagues in the field and in a research group.

The second story that needs to be mentioned is the way in which I conducted the investigation. I saw instances of student behavior that I chose not to follow. I chose not to explore the frictions between students because participant observation showed that the few instances I encountered were inconsequential to the bigger story of the adaptation to the program and the emergence of the GIite or GI person. The friction I witnessed or heard about did not have any heat. The students' conversations were mostly about coming to terms with the rigorous academic and residential demands of GI and about being an adolescent.

The story I have chosen to tell about student life in the Greenhouse Institute and the grounded theory that emerged were not obvious to me until a year after leaving the field. My increasing attention to student relationships and the honoring of diversity and excellence in the community system occurred after I recognized that my spontaneous reaction to questions like, "So, what have you learned?" was about those topics. I interpret my slow realization as an indication of an effort to shut out what was there because I feared my values might be pushing me in that direction. Two themes of my own life have been a commitment to social justice and democratic ideals and the desire to understand the experience of being gifted in modern society. The story I have written shows those life themes. Readers are warned to look for instances where the data do not warrant my interpretation. I wanted to tell a story of what was there, not of what I wanted to see.

Obviously, each student has his or her own story. I cannot tell all the stories. Instead, I try to capture what was there for most of the students. At the same time I selected a small number to illustrate the complexity of the Greenhouse Institute experience and give voice to their lives. If I have done that successfully, you will feel like you spent time in their shoes.

CHAPTER TWO

Being on Your Own in the Fast Lane

When juniors arrive for orientation, the newness is unsettling. As one student put it:

> I don't know how anybody who hasn't gone through it can understand it. In a half semester, I have gone through more stuff than I went through all last year. Just people, things happening, you are exposed to so much, so many new things all at once. It kind of blew my senses.

What is it that she has gone through that "blew her senses"? It is the relationships among students and adults within the physical setting and administrative organization of the school that create the meaning of the Greenhouse Institute (GI) for students. In order to appreciate the student experience at GI, we need to know who the people are that work and attend school there, why they came, and how they view the Greenhouse Institute.

STUDENTS CHOOSE THE FAST LANE

The Greenhouse Institute is a public, residential, 2-year high school. The students are juniors and seniors from around the state. They are from school districts that are under-resourced in urban and rural parts of the state; from wealthy suburbs and places becoming suburbs; and from families who are farmers, laborers, professionals, and service workers. GI students have three common characteristics that make them different from other students in the state. First, they choose to come to Greenhouse Institute. Public school students rarely choose what high school they attend. Second, the students define themselves as being "serious about learning." Most high school students do not say that about themselves. Third, the students are willing to go through an admission process 2 years before most high school students apply to college. In some cases, the students reported that their home schools were less than encouraging. During my first week at GI, two students shared stories of the uncooperativeness of their schools of origin. Theresa said her language teacher had been against her applying. "The teacher thinks leaving home is not worth the limited benefit of the school." The director of admissions echoed hearing such stories and noted that "getting the story out about the benefits of GI" was not easy.

The Application Process

Technically, GI applicants must submit portfolios that contain grades; test scores; recommendations from teachers of science, math, and humanities; an essay; and examples of work. However, the portfolios often contain more than is required. Applicants want to influence the admission process by standing out, so they submit portfolios with eye-catching decorations, graphics, and titles. One boy who expressed a strong interest in computers and had high science scores submitted poetry, stories, and essays in order to show that he is a very competent writer. In other folders I saw a letter of commendation from President Clinton, copies of awards for subject matter and athletic proficiency, stories clipped from local newspapers, pictures or detailed descriptions of projects, testimonials from hometown officials, a letter to the editor decrying nuclear weapons, a musical score, and videotapes.

The essay portion is a public statement of the student's reasons for applying. After reading a quarter of the portfolios of students who were accepted, their reasons fell into several obvious groupings. They wanted a challenge ("School now is a roadblock, my school is limiting me"; "I need a bigger challenge"; "I probably won't be relearning everything over and over"). Many students stated they wanted to be with peers who were serious about learning ("I need peers surrounding me who think as highly of academics as I do. I am sick of all the important time spent on students who joke around. . . . I want peers who are willing to have conversation"). Applicants also want to prepare for future goals and dreams ("I want to be ready for college"; "I want to be a doctor"). Some stated they wanted to have strong friendships ("At GI I can meet people and make friends for life").

Selection is made by a committee. A prime criterion is a sense that the student will fit in and thrive in the Greenhouse Institute's specialized environment. Students are not admitted solely on the basis of strong Scholastic Aptitude Test scores. While a high school sophomore with an SAT score of 950 but with great recommendations might be admitted, a student with an SAT score of 1300 who looked like he would not thrive in the environment might be rejected. Preview days are opportunities for the "prospectives" to visit GI and for the administration to examine the appropriateness of the fit between school and student. On Preview Day at lunch, two students were commenting on a prospective that had stayed in their room for most of the day: "He will never make it here." They saw the student as having too rigidly defined habits of sleeping and eating to meet the demands of life at GI.

Orientation

Much happens quickly on the orientation day. The E-shaped, three-story building has two wings branching out from a center area, with the boys' dorm on the right and the girls' dorm on the left. Welcoming signs are everywhere and people are milling around. At registration parents and students stand in lines before tables with signs that read CHECK IN, PICTURE, OFF-CAMPUS PERMISSIONS, HANDBOOK ACCEPTANCE AGREEMENT, NAME TAGS, BOOKS, PARENT BOOSTER CLUB, and so forth. A sea of brown-paper supermarket shopping bags labeled with names, overflowing with books for forthcoming classes, awaits students.

Once registration is complete, senior students who are Residence Assistants (RAs) help juniors find their Residence Counselor (RC). The RC greets the junior and shows him or her to his or her room. The RCs function as dorm parents and are supervised by the residential life director. Once a new student is shown to his or her room, the new roommate is met and the room is arranged to accommodate refrigerators, microwaves, TVs, VCRs, Nintendo, and all the other accoutrements of typical student life.

The rest of the day is spent learning more about the Greenhouse Institute. Convocations for family start the process in which the rules of living at GI are explained. As it gets close to 4:00 p.m., the time for saying good-bye approaches. Families will leave their children in the supervision of GI and the students will enter a new kind of life. Emotions are apparent. Juniors walk haltingly with their families to their vehicles. All look intense and uneasy as if no one wants to say the final words. Families work through the moment and to me they seem to be dancing in slow motion. Some families say good-bye quickly; others linger. There is much waving from the families as cars pull away. Students return to hall meetings with counselors who help them make sense of their new home.

INSTITUTIONAL HISTORY INFLUENCES STUDENTS' LIVES

The juniors enter an institution with a history that influences their experience indirectly. I heard repeated references to the past that were used to interpret the present even though the actors had changed. Casual and purposeful comments by adults and peers who are children of faculty bring information into the mix as meaning is constructed in the institute.

GI was rampant with bruised feelings connected to two past tragic events. One event was a suicide by a student. The other was a severe injury that occurred on a railroad trestle in a park near the school during students' free time. These events raised questions about supervision of student life.

IT NEVER STOPS, CHANGE IS EVERYWHERE

The feeling of transition, impermanence, and pace are not foremost in students' minds, even though signs are everywhere. Turnover in the student body due to graduation, withdrawal, and 24 hours crammed with activities generates in students feelings of change being everywhere. Much happens in 2 years. At graduation one half of the school leaves, and juniors become seniors. Juniors enter as seniors and begin preparing to leave for college.

Contributing to the students' sense of impermanence is the withdrawal of classmates from the school. "Choosing to withdraw" is the phrase adults use for students who leave voluntarily or are counseled out. However, students use phrases such as "kicked out" or "parents made her leave." The important fact about withdrawal is that friends and roommates may leave at any time. Regardless of the reason, students are remembered and rapidly lose currency in their peers' thoughts.

The pace of life at the school contributes to feelings of impermanence. Students refer to the energy and relentless demands. "Energy, there is so much energy here. People are up talking, it never stops." "More happens in one week here than in a whole month at my old school!" The fullness and pace is due to academic and residential demands making it hard for students to catch their breath.

WHO OWNS THE KIDS?

The two staffs—teachers and counselors—share a belief in the mission of GI yet hold differing views about what the mission means. These conflicts produce the foundational struggle between adults at GI, which is captured by the question, Who owns the kids? I use the term *foundational* because the struggle is pervasive, profound, and potentially lethal to the school. In this section I highlight the uneasy, entangled coexistence of Academic Life (AL) and Residential Life (RL) and leave more subtle points until Chapters 6 and 8.

The two major divisions believe they have the best interests of the students in mind. This struggle for who owns the kids is the natural antipathy built into their roles of teacher and counselor. The residence counselors (RC) are selected for a "holistic orientation" and are concerned with the "whole person." RCs believe that children should have balanced and adjusted lives. Feelings are their stock in trade. The students unsettle them by their attention to studying and willingness to put aside social activities for that purpose. In a program that selects on the basis of academic pursuit, an RC may tell some kids to stop studying for a while. Counselors appreciate the teacher's role and respect their knowledge. They regard faculty commitment to their subject to be misplaced when the students obviously have other unmet needs and are in psychological risk or danger. RCs interpret teachers' willingness to stay late and work with students to be an infringement on the students' need for nonacademic activities, even though that is not the view of the students. The RCs view students as adolescents in a residential setting who have the same needs as regular high school kids. They believe the students could not survive without them.

The teachers are hired for their academic expertise and regard themselves as being the reason for the school's existence. Teachers assume that the students will be as committed as they are to their fields. The counselors must facilitate students' academic development. As far as teachers are concerned, their subject, among all curricular subjects, comes first. Counselors should be monitoring the students to direct them to a "life of the mind." The teachers generally see the RCs as young people who are well intentioned, appreciate their role, and consider them as not being far from the maturity level of the students. RCs are often viewed as indulging the students. Teachers believe that a counselor's reason-for-being is to support the academic program. The teachers find it unbelievable that an RC would tell a student to ease off studying and unimaginable that to do so would be a good thing. Many teachers have close relationships with students because they share a love of the subject matter or the course. RCs have trouble understanding relationships based on a shared love of the subject matter because their experience as students is not comparable. The exceptions are counselors who have either been at the school as students or have devoted themselves to developing their own talents.

The pervasive reality of the split between teachers and residence counselors is both overt and subtle. Despite administrative efforts, the conflict reemerges. The most striking incident occurred at dinner one evening away from the institute. In a mixed counselor and teacher group, one teacher remarked that some fellow teachers would regard the speaker as a "traitor" for socializing with the counselors.

INFORMATION IS PRIVILEGED

The Greenhouse Institute is a closed system in that information about any student is contained primarily within the physical boundaries of the place, which means that the meanings held by students and adults are developed there. Information at GI is privileged and private. The root of the school's policy of confidentiality was interpretations of state law and professional ethics. The underlying rule is as follows: Unless there is a clear need to have information about a student's actions, academic status, psychological status, or family status to deal with a current situation, you will not be told. Ironically, confidentiality produces a distorting effect on the GI social climate.

The policy on confidentiality was applied to grades. At GI grades are not posted. No one knows how a student fared unless the student decides to share that information. Students may create a story about how they are doing in school without contrary evidence.

One incident stands out in my mind that illustrates what can happen. A young man was advised to withdraw. Neither students nor the faculty knew the complete story of what had precipitated the request. The student told his peers that he was doing well. Some students, rallying to his defense, raised the issue of his race being connected to the dismissal. The faculty, upset by this situation, could not supply contrary information. A few weeks later, the student withdrew. A minority student and I were in a local coffee bar sharing experience about living in the dorm. I asked how it felt when a roommate or friend left. The student, speaking about the student who had withdrawn, startled me with the remark, "There are so many white kids doing just as well as he was and they were not asked to withdraw." The intensity of the comment pushed me to observe that he looked lost in a math class we were in together. Instead of mollifying the situation, it sparked, "Minority men are systematically discriminated against in our society. I thought GI was not like the rest of the world!"

This one instance illustrates how confidentiality can have a positive intention yielding negative side effects. GI has worked hard to retain the student using tutors, a contract, and so forth. The actual level of student performance was not known. The student conveyed an inflated portrait of his performance. Racism raised its ugly head and no meaningful response emerged. The incident dramatically shows how the policies of the institution can distort normal social relations in the school and thus influence the life of students.

ORGANIZATIONAL SETTING

The Greenhouse Institute is located in a corner of the university among a complex of buildings. GI shares land with a lab school run by the College of Education, a dining hall building, and the GI dorm. The dorm is the only building to which it has sole access; the others are shared.

The mission of the Greenhouse Institute is "to provide a healthy and challenging residential community for eleventh- and twelfth-grade students of high academic ability who are committed to reaching their full potential with a holistic framework" (Greenhouse Institute, 1996, p. 1). At the same time the Greenhouse Institute is supposed to assist "other high schools across the state for quality staff development, distance learning and support services" (p. 1).

The statement of philosophy in the faculty handbook reads:

> The curriculum of the Greenhouse Institute is designed to provide a balance between the study of required subjects from traditional disciplines and the opportunity for individual exploration and personal enrichment. Throughout the curriculum, the processes of critical thinking, creativity, problem-solving, research, and decision-making are stressed. . . . Established . . . by the legislature, the Greenhouse Institute is . . . devoted to the education of students who demonstrate extraordinary intellectual ability and a commitment to scholarship. The philosophy of the Greenhouse Institute originates from the proposition that a society in which justice is a prime concern ordinarily tries to provide educational opportunities appropriate to the expressed ability and potential development of as many sorts of citizens as possible. . . . The Greenhouse Institute is dedicated to inspiring and challenging highly gifted young adults to reach their full potential within a framework of the common good. (Greenhouse Institute, 1996, p. 6)

The administrative structure of GI has three divisions: Academic Life, Residential Life, and Outreach. Other functions are subsumed under those headings. Academic Life and Residential Life most directly influence students. They are discussed more in depth in later chapters. Outreach, however, is largely invisible to students. An executive director heads the Greenhouse Institute and directors lead each of the three divisions. Essentially, these four people run the school.

Academic Life (AL) contains all the activities related to delivering a rigorous academic program. AL is composed of one director, teachers of various subjects, a guidance counselor, and a support staff. Academic Life is defined by the honors curriculum that is required by the state as carried out by the instructors. The curriculum is broken into science, math, computer applications, humanities, and languages. Teachers who are experts in their fields teach classes. Students are expected to be serious about learning. The courses are fast-paced, with heavy homework demands.

Several aspects of academic life make GI different from regular high schools. First, the courses are offered on a collegelike schedule. Classes are not taught every day, although the length of a class is still one hour. This puts pressure on the teachers to get in all the required content in fewer contact hours than is usual in high schools. The faculty has office hours in the late afternoons and evenings so that students can drop in any time.

Residential Life (RL) is that part of the institute that occurs outside of Academic Life. RL is composed of one director, two dorm assistants who head the female and male sides, residence counselors, and a counseling psychologist. RL presents itself as the emotional part of the school. Students spend most of their day under the supervision of Residential Life. It is responsible for attending to the nonacademic needs of students and for enforcing the various rules and regulations that characterize the place. The arenas for which they are responsible are recreation, food, free time, living arrangements, sleeping, health needs, extracurricular needs outside of school, the Wellness program, and so forth. RCs carry out the policies of the division. RCs live in the dorm in their own small apartments surrounded by their charges. Each RC has one or more Residence Assistants, seniors who assist them in their role. The students expect the RC to be available when they need him or her.

The Outreach division provides educational services to other schools in the state. The Admissions Office, which is responsible for recruiting students, is a part of Outreach. Many students feel a bond with this office because it provided their first contact with GI. When asked, "Who do you know?", students mentioned the person(s) who recruited them more than any other staff member. The Career and College Counseling Office, also a part of Outreach, offers a supportive environment for students seeking the best postsecondary school for them. Students are helped to prepare college applications.

The GI administration sets the official schedule of the school in accordance with the rules of the state board of education and the board of the university in which it resides. The GI yearly schedule includes normal holidays plus extended weekends (when students go home for a long weekend). The weekly academic schedule is organized like a college. Classes meet for 3 days, except for classes with labs (such as language classes), which meet for 4 days. Classes begin at 8:00 a.m. and continue into the late afternoon. Most are over by 4:00 p.m. At 6:30 p.m., mandatory study hours begin. After study hours end at 8:00 p.m., students may leave the GI buildings with another student until 10:00 p.m. By 10:30 p.m., every student is supposed to be on his or her floor where he or she can study or visit with friends. By 12:30 a.m., lights are supposed to be off and students asleep.

CONCLUSION

The stage has been set in this chapter for the story of the students' experience in a 2-year, state-sponsored, residential high school designed to promote the development of academic talent. Students separate themselves from other high school students in the state by announcing their seriousness about learning and choosing to apply to a school away from their home school. Going through a cumbersome application process, they join a highly talented group of learners in an environment filled with adults who want to help them develop their talent.

CHAPTER THREE

The Heart of the Greenhouse Institute

Living in the fast lane expresses the essence of the GI experience. Students are carried forward by the academic and nonacademic demands toward graduation. Enter one year, leave the next, keep your foot on the accelerator.

Students characterized life at GI using six attributes: fluidity, "openness," acceptance, "shock and amazement," busy, and "pressure." (The quoted terms students use; the others are my succinct interpretations.) "Openness" means that all kinds of ideas are floating around in conversations and classes. Fluidity means that relationships change, with permeable boundaries between groups. Acceptance means that expressing various sorts of behaviors, ranging from conforming to idiosyncratic, is okay. Busy means that days are filled with activities, deadlines are ever present, and one is usually on the verge of moving on to another activity. "Pressure" means that the pace of life is amplified and accelerated by academic requirement, the intensity of dorm life, and conceptions of self. "Shock and amazement" refers to the reaction students have when they encounter diversity, rigorous academics, and the limits of residential life. They learn they are in a place compared to which "nothing else is close."

Living in the fast lane means rushing forward into life, seeking out new ideas, and trying new behaviors as fast as possible toward some elusive state of being that keeps changing. Three of the characteristics—pressure, busy, fluidity—imply speed and movement. The phrase "shock and amazement" describes the attractiveness and the emotional allure of the place. The two remaining characteristics—openness and acceptance—imply meeting new and challenging ideas that call for continuous change and rapid adjustment.

The intersection of student and school yields an excitingly seductive setting where students are compelled to grow and move forward. The GI pull is intrusive. During their free time, whether students are hanging out, sleeping, or simply daydreaming, thoughts of having to do something are always present.

"Life in the fast lane" does not describe a typical high school. The Greenhouse Institute is an *atypical* high school. The contrast is evident in two competing educational models of educating talented and gifted children: Talent Multiple Abilities Model and Whole Child Model (Coleman & Cross, 2001). Within the GI elements of both models are present as an undercurrent in the friction between the counselors and teachers. The Greenhouse Institute resembles the Talent Multiple Ability Model because GI wants to develop academic talent. On the other hand, the Whole Child Model strives to develop all aspects of children, as is the mission of a typical comprehensive high school. The contrast between other high schools in the state where GI is located, and GI, is represented in Table 3.1. Obviously, variation among the state's high schools is much broader than Table 3.1 illustrates.

Several differences stand out. The residential versus nonresidential nature of the schools is the most obvious. Having an influence on student behavior for 24 hours is much different than only having such an influence for 6 hours. The creation of a special setting is another strong difference, as is the high value placed on academic learning. In the typical high school academics are valued, but the structure is not specifically organized to do that primarily. GI offers extracurricular and athletic activities, but have far less importance than the academic program. The Greenhouse Institute has no football or other major team sports. Finding a high school without a major sport team is impossible in the state. Following this point, GI starts with the assumption that students will be committed to academic learning. It is expected; developing such a commitment is not a goal. Devoting oneself to doing academics is everywhere; in fact, devoting oneself to any academic interest is considered highly appropriate. Other differences are the presence of diversity and the value of individuality. GI is more diverse than the typical high schools in the state, so GI students meet many others who are not like them. Expressions of individuality and individual differences are welcomed. Acceptance is seen not only in the commitment to academic projects, but also in personal matters such as artistic expression and sexual orientation.

A subtle but major difference between the typical high school and the Greenhouse Institute is the lack of knowledge people have about you as a person at the start. At GI most enter with no history. The influence of your family and the past has no bearing on status at GI. What you become, not who you are, is the predominant value.

WHAT IS GI?

As part of my research strategy, I asked open-ended questions such as, "What stands out in your mind about GI?" and "GI is like . . . ?" Their responses

Table 3.1. Comparing GI to a Typical Local High School

Greenhouse Institute	Typical Local High School
Diversity is evident, actively encouraged	Diversity is rare, policy is encouraged
Permeable boundaries among groups	Definite boundaries among groups
Individuality in ideas and dress is okay	Collectivity is the rule, some behavior is out
New clubs can be formed easily	Clubs can be formed
Nominal groups (clubs) that expand and contract	
Acceptance that one might have contradictory interests	Discomfort with contradictory interests
Residential setting	Does not apply
Frequency of contact throughout the day	Frequency of contact primarily at school
Encouraged not to be isolated, but it is okay	Encouraged not to be isolated, worry if so
"Busyness" and/or pressure to learn is expected	Doing what is required is expected
Transition: every year one half leaves	Transition: every year one fourth go
No one stays more than 2 years	Most stay 4 years
Significant number of withdrawals	Significant dropouts
No history to trail you	History in town and school
Few have family history in school	Many have family history in school
Most fellow students are not known before entry	Many fellow students are known
No relatively fixed hierarchy of status in place	Relatively stable hierarchy in place
Assignment to social categories is created, flexible	Assignment to social categories is preexistent and stable
Few athletic teams, no football team	Many teams

anchor this chapter and my story of life in the fast lane. Four defining aspects of the Greenhouse Institute stood out to students: diversity, homework, residential life, and the addictive quality of life.

Diversity Is Everywhere

Meeting diversity face-to-face is one of the first things that stand out to students about their experience at the Greenhouse Institute. Most students come from schools with little or no diversity. "Absolutely no diversity" was a frequent comment. Some students chose to come to GI because they heard it was more diverse. The mix of students amazes even those who were seeking diversity. A female junior remarked that diversity "is great for me because my old school was all White, just one Black. I came here and it's just amazing. My roommate is Korean, one of my best friends is black, so [there's] a lot of opportunity." Living together with diverse others increases chances for becoming familiar with differing lifestyles. All students reported friendships with people whom they may not have been friendly with at their home high school. A Black senior smiled and shook his head with a disbelieving look as he admitted that he was friendly with "Goths and gays," something he would never have done at home.

The Greenhouse Institute may be the most diverse school in the state. It should be noted that at GI diversity means more than just racial variations. Other descriptors of diversity are geographic (urban, suburban, rural), socioeconomic (parents who are doctors, farmers, service workers, welfare recipients), length of residency in America (immigrant children, second generation, 5th generation), sexual orientation (gay, bisexual, straight), religious affiliation (Roman Catholics, Lutherans, Jains, Hindus, Muslims, Buddhists), and academic self-definition (I am a science person, a math person, or a humanities person).

Encountering diversity is not the same as liking diversity or being comfortable with diversity. Discomfort is a common emotion new students experience when arriving at GI. More often than not this yields to acceptance and frequently to comfort:

> I think that generally diversity is a very good thing here. I'm so happy that I'm exposed to [it] in addition to just Black culture . . . most Americans conceptualize America as being Black and White. They're just not Black and White. There's Indian, and there's Persian, and there's Chinese and Japanese.

The aspect of diversity that is most challenging for students is the presence of gay and lesbian peers. In their home schools, expressions of homophobia were the norm. At GI students learn to reconcile negative, religious-based sentiments learned at home and the presence of a likable peer with a sexual orientation outside the homebound norms:

> Because of my religion, I don't think it's right to be homosexual, but I don't think it's right to hate people either. I don't think it's right to say well they're a homosexual, they're automatically and completely evil and that I shouldn't hang around them. But at the same time, I don't know.

Race is not spoken of as a criterion for friendship. White students say there is no racism and remark that diversity is a common discussion topic. The Wellness program in residential life (to be described later) encourages this attitude. White students believe the school policy would not sanction racist or homophobic comments. This might influence the frequency of open comments. My informants told me of jokes and teasing that might be inferred as racist, yet I recall hearing none in my wanderings. The conventional responses to such racist comments is, "Shut up now," "We don't want to hear it," and "You shouldn't say that." The students have friendships that are much more diverse because there are opportunities here that do not exist at home, which they like. As one senior said,

> My mom quilts, and my grandma does too. She has like rag quilts she makes from old things, like old dresses, or old bedspreads, or old sheets . . . And that's what I thought the Greenhouse Institute was like because . . . we all come from very different places and I know that I am nothing like any of these girls in this room, except that somebody somewhere thought that I was gifted so they thought that I should come here. And I think that that's neat that like we were all thrown together, and now we all get to explore and see what kinds of different groups and friends and ideas that we can have when we meet. You know? That's what I was thinking. That's what I think the best quality of GI is the diversity I guess.

Students who are Black value diversity, too. Like their White counterparts, they were the dominant group in their home schools. As members of a minority group within the larger society, they have more experience dealing with different others than do the White students. The Black students seem to have an either-or approach to same-race friendships. One either spends a lot of time with racial peers or relatively little time with them. This duality seemed true for both boys and girls. Race is not spoken of as the most important determinant of friendship, but it is an important variable for some, especially the Black girls. Black girls spend more time with other Black girls than the Black boys do with other Black boys. Unlike their nonblack peers, African-American students say racism is present, yet less so than in the world outside GI. Black students notice that racism is avoided by White students as a topic of discussion and they interpret events as examples of racism that their White counterparts would not.

Asian voices are more varied than those of Caucasians and African Americans. The variety among Asian groups makes generalization tenuous. Indian males stand out as a group, like the Black females, in that all notice they separate themselves at meals. Anyone can join them, but they tend to stay apart. Interestingly, they are not the same because their ancestral ties are from different states of India which do not speak the same language or even have the same religion.

The diversity of the student body is important to the Greenhouse Institute administration. The receptivity of the students to the presence of diversity is fed by the philosophy of the school that creates a supportive setting for all varieties of children. From the welcoming words of the director at orientation, to the Wellness program of residential life that offers credit for having multicultural experiences, to the formation of extracurricular clubs, diversity is respected. GI has a system that permits students with a faculty sponsor to form clubs to meet specialized interests. Several clubs are support groups for diverse students. Membership is open to all students. For example, the Black Students League is a large club with Black and White membership. Other clubs, such as the Indian Club, the Persian Club, and so forth, follow this pattern. While attending various club meetings, I observed diversity in action. In one meeting a White student helped organize a Black awareness program. In another, Indian students were planning a dinner to share foods. During the discussion, members realized that they did not understand the nature of food dishes that were being described because of the variety of Indian subcultures.

Rigorous Academics Is New

A second startling part of the experience of being at the Greenhouse Institute is the rigorous academic program. Students choose to come for the academics, yet few are prepared for what they find. Two aspects of academic life contribute to this feeling: the amount of homework and the teachers.

The relentless homework demand throws some students off balance. Many have never had to study and few really know how to do it. Before GI, homework was something you fit in and coordinated with your social life. A major part of the adjustment to life at GI is learning that academic demands come first and social interests come second. Staying at GI requires this equation. These changes are shocking to students and some resist it.

Meeting teachers who are experts and who want to share their knowledge is another change for new GI students. Many are struck by the availability of teachers and their interest in the students. "They really listen to you." Part of this is facilitated by the teachers' evening office hours. The relationships with teachers are one of the aspects of GI that stand out for graduating seniors. One girl said her image of GI is "sitting in Miss Van Pelt's office talking and working on homework assignments and projects." Students commonly stop off at a teacher's office to say hello and talk. This is a pleasant shock.

RESIDENTIAL LIFE

Leaving home and living with strangers under a set of rules stands out to many students as the dominant feature of life at the Greenhouse Institute. Those who have been to camp find this situation to be less stressful. Students must confront major changes in their daily lives. The informality, negotiation, and attention to one as an individual, which is characteristic of family life, is replaced by a broad set of rules governing conduct, administered by strangers, in an institutional-feeling dorm. One is clearly in a different home. The relationships between students and adults are unfamiliar. One's roommate is often a stranger with different values, routines, and ethnicity. The loss of privacy bothers some. I heard the expression, "people know what you are doing" as an indication of the public nature of relationships. The adults say the set of rules exists for "protecting the students," but students say they exist for "limiting our freedom." Wellness, a residential life program that is intended to help students manage their lives and develop a broader perspective on life, requires them to participate in activities "for our own good!" Clashes occur over the rules and Wellness. This friction underlies all of residential life. Some students resist it mightily. Others dislike it and acquiesce. The rest barely seem to notice. Those who bristle under the limits on behavior see GI as being restrictive. In those cases, "minimum security prison" or some similar metaphor is used when referring to residential life.

THE ADDICTIVE QUALITY OF LIFE IN THE FAST LANE

The fourth aspect of GI life that stands out is its addictive quality. Although I heard no student use the term *addictive* directly, I heard much about becoming swept up in the fullness of the days and the challenges of academic and residential life. Comments such as, "So much happens here," "It is like no place else in the world," "You are always near a friend," and "It feels like home" are testimonies to the student experience. When there are long weekends or vacations, new students eagerly head home to relax and see family and friends. But before long, many students wish they were back again when they are away, and are eager to return. The combination of academic and residential life produces a potent, potentially addictive stew. For many, the Greenhouse Institute becomes their home, the place where they belong and can be themselves.

RHYTHMS OF THE GREENHOUSE INSTITUTE

GI students have the opportunity to have busy lives. They live in an environment that is rich with activities and events—both organized and spontaneous, required and informal—with which one can become engaged. Activities start before breakfast and go well into the night. In some cases, activities can extend into the early morning hours. As the day progresses, the number of choices escalate, as does the competition among personal interests, academic requirements, and desires.

Repeating patterns are the building blocks of a schedule. They are the baseline within the rhythm of the day. The strongest rhythmic force is the official academic schedule. The week has three distinct riffs or patterns: Monday and Wednesday, Tuesday and Thursday, and the weekend. The tone of the Greenhouse Institute is really different on those days. Monday and Wednesday are serious days, quick-time kind of days. People rise earlier, scurry to classes, and finish assignments in spare time. The evening is a little wilder, more undisciplined because the next day has lighter classes. Tuesday and Thursday are more laid back, slow-time kind of days. Bigger blocks of free time appear. One sees more roughhousing, more hanging out in the lounges throughout the day. People wake later and do homework. These days serve for catching up and preparing for the next day. By evening students are thinking about the next busy day and doing homework. Friday is a less serious day than Monday and Wednesday because the weekend follows. Weekends bring the slowest time. Many anticipate leaving and others look forward to taking it easy. Time stretches out and slows down. Study hours are not required and dinner slides into evening. Saturday and Sunday rising happens near or after lunchtime. Many stay in their rooms resting, studying, and hanging out. The weekend is the time to rest up for the new week. By Sunday late afternoon, attention turns to the new week and the beat speeds up.

Class Patterns

The basic number of classes that students attend depends on state requirements for high school graduation with honors, GI-specific requirements, and
students' interests. The curriculum offers a variety of courses. Classes extend from 8:00 a.m. to 4:00 p.m., with a few having later classes. Monday,
Wednesday, and Friday are the heavy class days. Most courses are offered
in a building near the dorm and a small number around the university.

Residential Life Patterns

Not-in-class time falls under the purview of RL. These periods of time are
segmented by the time of day and the expected activity.

The Late Afternoon, Before Dinner. Lasting from 3:00 or 4:00 to 5:30,
most students unwind from classes. At this point Residential Life programming overlaps Academic Life programming. Some classes are scheduled in
time frames that conflict with nonacademic activities such as field trips, rehearsals, and so on. An example would be that Astronomy class interferes
with a chance to play Ultimate Frisbee. A relatively small number of students are involved in intramural or school team sports.

Three Official Meals. Students choose to eat in the dining hall. Breakfast has the smallest number, lunch the most, and dinner a little less than
lunch. Eating occurs when it fits into one's schedule. A small number of students actually leave to go eat at local restaurants or in their rooms.

Required Study Hours. Studying is done with the doors closed, a
new procedure that gives students the chance to do what they want and
be "invisible." Some study, some sleep, and some listen to music. Despite
the fact that this is a preserved time period, there are many incursions into
the territory, such as tutoring another student, participating in sports (volleyball, track), play practices, or meeting service requirements (discussed
in Chapter 6).

Evenings Before Dorm Hours. Study time concludes at 8:00 p.m. At
this juncture many choices are possible. Many students choose to continue
studying. Students also use this time to do nonacademic activities such as
leaving the building. Often leaving is simply "to get away" from GI for a
while and to "hang out." Ordinarily, about 30% of students hide out and
engage in this unlawful activity during this time.

Dorm Hours. Hall hours start at 10:00, or 10:30 for seniors, and students are expected to be up on their floors at this time. It ends at 12:30 when students must return to their rooms. However, it is possible that a committee or club, such as the Prom Committee or Students for Radical Change at GI, is meeting. More studying takes place at this time than at earlier points in the evening. The social and the academic merge at this time; studying might be paired with talking, video gaming, watching videos, or eating. Movement occurs up and down floors with permission of the Residential Counselor (RC) until lights out.

Sleep Time. The least likely thing to happen at 12:30 a.m. when students are supposed to sleep is for lights to go out. Large numbers prepare for bed. The floors become quiet. Students wait in their rooms until they can leave without drawing the attention of the RC and play video games or talk with their friends. Some students retire to the designated study lounges on each floor to do work without disturbing their roommates.

SOLOISTS PLAY THEIR OWN TUNE

Four GI students—Tracie, Marvin, Samir, and Wanda—have schedules that are representative of life in the fast lane. These students are met again later.

Tracie

Tracie, a senior, feels pressure from time to time, but generally she gets everything done and loves GI. Her typical Monday and Tuesday schedule illustrates her style.

Tracie's alarm rings at 7:15 a.m. She jumps into her clothes, which are folded beside my bed. "I do not like to miss breakfast before my four classes [Statistics, Literature, Civilization, Chinese]." Tracie eats lunch at noon, "but sometimes if I have a paper to type or something I'd skip lunch to take care of it." She has British Lit. at 1:00, which is "a class I love." A break between 2:00 and 3:00 allows her time to read the new Brit Lit. assignment, either in her room or in the lounge. Anatomy class is at 3:00. "That ends my class day." Back in the dorm at 4:00, she talks with her RC, then reads or cleans up her room. "My roommate and I go to dinner at 4:30, talking about the day with anyone who joins us." Returning near 5:30, Tracie hangs out in the dorm room and may study or work on a project. When study session begins at 6:30, she chooses either to study straight through, talk to her roommate, or watch movies. "And at eight o'clock, if I'm feeling adventurous, I'll venture out of the building with my roommate and we'll go for a walk or go to Revco (drug-store). Usually we are back in the building by about nine o'clock." Hanging out in the lounge or in her RC's apartment talking is her routine, but if pressed she returns to her room to study. "At about ten-thirty, I shower and am in bed by twelve-thirty, reading until 1:00." On Tuesday she has one class. She completes homework and/or works at a Pizza Hut on campus. For the rest of the day, she tutors and does homework. "Because I have senior privilege I can eat later and not have [a] study session. When an RC will let us, several of us, girls and boys, hang out watching our favorite soap opera until the end of study session. Often, I have a club meeting or something to do before ten."

Marvin

Marvin does not do all the academic assignments because "I want a social life." Marvin usually goes to bed anytime after 1:00 a.m., then rises at 6:30 to shower, dress, and go to breakfast by 7:30. He has two classes (American Lit. and Computer Applications) followed by a break at 10:00. "So I eat lunch at ten-thirty." Then he has four classes (Physics, Precalculus, Civilization, and Spanish) in two buildings across campus. "By 3:00, my schedule is cool. I come back, chill out in the boy's lounge, check my e-mail, and maybe do a little homework, if motivated, until I check in at four o'clock with my RC upstairs." Marvin eats between 5:00 and 6:00 and is back for a study session in which he either sleeps or studies. "On Monday, Wednesday, and Friday, I leave the building at eight. There is not much homework the next day and I need to get away and be social. We walk around the campus or go to the Village [a local strip of stores, fast food, and bars]. It is hard to have any privacy here." By 10:00 p.m., he is in the lounge. "Immediately, I head for my friend Sam's room until 12:30 because I don't like being in my room. We talk and study." Sometimes he studies in his room until around 2:00. "On Tuesday I have a physics lab from ten to twelve so I wake up at eight-thirty and skip breakfast." On Thursday he has junior research class. "After that I eat lunch, and do whatever. By night I am doing homework, often in computer lab, because Wednesday is a heavy day." Marvin is not a member of any clubs.

Samir

Samir, too, has a hectic schedule, one that is made even more so by his allegiance to his roots. He works until he runs out of energy.

Samir wakes up at 6:30, after going to bed about 1:00, "so I can shower undisturbed and dress." Having prepacked his bag before bed, he goes to the dining hall at 7:30. For the next 5 hours he has classes. "In between Physics and Chinese, I drop by the dining hall to pick up a sack lunch." This requires that he make a special arrangement ahead of time. This arrangement enables him to eat or nap at 1:00 p.m. "Here, you learn to fall asleep quickly." Samir has American Lit. and Civilization from 2:00 to 4:00. "I calculate that if I read between classes, I can add an hour plus to my homework time during the day. I always try to finish my homework because we finish what we start in my family." By 4:00 he checks e-mail, plays a computer game, reports to his RC, and does a little homework. At 5:30 he and his roommate go to the dining hall. Returning around 6:15, they pass the teachers' offices to say hello or ask questions before the 6:30 study time. "I study pretty much the whole session, but I sometimes tutor at this time. I like to follow the rules." Samir studies until 8:00, when he leaves for the gym to do some "lifting" (weights). Returning to the dorm, "I may talk to some friends in the lounge or my room. I study in my room from ten until one or when I fall asleep. I find myself staying up later and later as the semester goes on." Tuesday follows a similar pattern. He has two classes, Colloquia and Physics Lab. "I study during free time. At night I socialize less because Wednesday is a heavy class day." Samir also belongs to three clubs, which meet on intermittent evenings at various times. "The weekend allows me to sleep and recover from the week of work."

Wanda

Wanda harbors doubts about belonging and fitting in to the GI life, yet she wants to stay, too. Wanda's Monday begins at 2:00 a.m. when she goes to sleep after studying on Sunday night. Five and a half hours later, she dresses quickly and hurries to her 8:00 American Lit. class while munching on a donut. Five classes follow quickly (German, Precalculus, Physics). Astronomy is across campus, so she rushes to lunch at 1:00. After eating, Wanda checks her e-mail and barely arrives in time for her 2:00 Civilization class. Her classes end at 3:00, so she has 2 hours to "go back to my room and listen to music for an hour before going downstairs to the lounge at four to play foosball." She eats in the dining hall at five. Routinely, she stays in the lounge until six-thirty. "I have a different mind-set when I am not in class. During study session I listen to music, sleep infrequently, and maybe study [if pushed by a major reading assignment]." As soon as it is permitted, Wanda walks with friends "just to get away from GI. My workload influences whether I return in one or two hours. I go directly to my room to start studying until twelve." On Tuesday, she awakens later for her two classes. After lunch, physics homework is done before the 2-hour lab. The second semester on Thursday was a no-class day.

CONCLUSION

Tracie, Marvin, Samir, and Wanda provide glimpses into students' daily routines and some of their personal styles. Significant aspects of life in the fast lane come into focus. The busy scheduled 24-hour days of GI life are shaped by rigorous academic demands and the rules and requirements governing residential life. The quick pace of life is heightened by the students' own intensity and repeated contact with diverse people and ideas. The result is a faster pace stimulating environment, and that becomes addictive.

Understanding the full story of students' experience in the GI community requires keeping these broad attributes in mind as we examine life more microscopically in the academic and residential divisions of GI.

Learning and Academic Life

The first thing new students must learn is either to adapt to the fast-paced environment or leave. Students master large chunks of information and tidbits of tacit knowledge about academics that they were unlikely to learn at home. The content eases their transition to college. Students assert that they learn to study, most for the first time. Challenge becomes something one learns to take in stride. The complexity of various intellectual and social issues becomes apparent. Students learn to write better, too.

Yet much beyond academics is learned in the context of school life. Some of it is positive, some of it useful, and some of it may be potentially maladaptive. Students learn to find time for nonacademic activities in the rigorous academic environment. A sizable number become excited about learning again; many confirm that they can continue on the path to the career they want. Students develop a sense of their own agency by learning that they can interact and compete with bright peers who are from diverse races, religions, and ethnicities. Who they may be in the future becomes less fuzzy. Some learn they have limits, may not be as smart as they thought they were, and can be successful students, too. Most learn how to handle feeling overloaded and manage their time.

Students learn how to survive and many thrive in the intense academically rigorous environment. For some that means learning how to postpone social relationships for a long-range goal. They learn to meet the stringent academic demands by completing portions of an assignment, faking what they have not read, getting time extensions to cover their procrastination, and accepting lower grades. Most learn how to outwit rules that restrict their choices. They learn how to work with those in authority to circumvent unrealistic demands. All learn to sleep fast and work for deadlines. All learn to be independent of their families and to live with others who are not family members.

WHAT ACADEMICALLY RIGOROUS REALLY MEANS

The rigorous academic program is something for which new students are unprepared. Academic loads are much heavier than anticipated. One junior said it for her peers: "The difficulty of classes is all-around. It is just a shock to actually have to study, do homework, to like do more than a few minutes a class." Students experience a sharp departure from prior experience that is amplified by the regimen of GI. Homework takes time, is ever-present, and is never quite finished. For most new students, their local high schools called for little to no studying. "There was just no homework, really," said one student.

The Greenhouse Institute is different. A junior explained what it meant to be at GI for her and for others.

> It's so serious and you have to work to get all this done, you have to have an honors diploma, you have to work a lot harder to get good grades. At home I never did it. I did my homework all in class and I got straight A's. Here, I do homework and I study and I get mostly B's. You know, you have to work a lot harder. It's more stressful. And so the ability just to go out, have fun, leave school and not have to worry about homework, about what's due the next day, and about how many papers are due that week, you know?

Her statement implies two changes in her life. First, homework becomes a major presence and the quantity of studying increases beyond expectations. Second, the balance changes between the academic and social routines of high school life. Attending to friends and nonacademic interests that was the pattern of the past is reshaped by the worry over finishing homework for the next day and further on. In other words, the way in which a student spends a day and how he or she thinks about that day can change. Together, these changes converge to produce an initial feeling of shock that lessens over the year. For some students the pattern remains disturbing because of "the inescapable problem of coming from an environment where homework was much less and having the urge to socialize."

HOMEWORK IS CALLING

Rarely does a student not have outstanding homework. This heightens feeling pressured. The relentless quality of homework is expressed in the following vivid metaphor by a junior:

It's just like you are standing in the ocean waiting for the next wave to hit, and on the weekend you crawl back up the beach, and you rest and on Monday you go out and stand again.

Having to do homework is only part of the story. That ever-present feeling is magnified by the apprehension that studying is not a set of skills that they possess. Learning how to study is more upsetting than the homework load.

I had the worst time learning how to study, because it was just something I had never done. I'd not read, not done homework, just pay attention in class and get A's on tests. And that was like school for me until I got here. And I was like, a paper, why would I have to write a paper!? Or do homework?

—a female senior

Some students actually welcome the increased academic demands. For these students, learning how to study was pleasantly unsettling. Some arrived at GI as successful students who had lost, or put aside, their early interest in learning. The challenging nature of homework that required thinking rekindled their interest in learning for its own sake.

HOMEWORK AND STUDYING ARE NOT SYNONYMS

The students and I often used the words *homework* and *studying* interchangeably. However, most students make a distinction between homework and studying. The way in which any student regards homework appears to be linked to a sense of self. Three statements about homework reverberate with meaning. The order of the statements parallels the frequency of the expression: Most students would agree with the first statement but relatively few students would agree with the last statement. The separation between statements one and three points toward the very different ways that students experience the Greenhouse Institute. The three statements follow.

Homework Is Done During the Day, Studying Is Done at Night. During the day when they are not in class, students may spend their time doing last-minute preparation for class or quick naps. Immediacy and short-term intervals drive this statement. Little studying is done during the day; most of it occurs on Tuesdays and Thursdays. Relatively little studying is done on Mondays and Wednesdays because the schedule is too busy and compact. This statement is more a statement of process than of self. A female senior stated, "You do not have time to do what you want to do. You've got to do what you need to do to graduate and you've got a few options."

Homework Is Due Next Class, Studying Is Done Later. Homework that will be collected and checked is attended to first. That immediacy gives way to the need to have more time to complete some homework so one can think about the assignment. Again, the time available and the nature of the assignment interact. Projects take more time and thought, so they are done on Tuesday, Thursday, and weekends when time is available. Heavy reading assignments that occur in the Humanities course often fall into this group. These are often done in the evening or other times when there are uninterrupted blocks of time available. Students slip away to quiet spaces to read.

Homework I Do for the School, Studying I Do for Me. This statement was heard almost verbatim from seniors, male and female, who volunteered it. The insertion of self into the third statement makes it much different than the preceding two. An implication is that homework is an institutionally linked event that may or may not have personal relevance. Studying, on the other hand, has more of a personal quality. A female senior explained how she thought about it in a way that echoes other participants in this study:

> Because I've learned like I personally have to have time for me, I cannot stay in this building all the time to do all of my homework . . . I have learned that I, as a person, as a human, need time for myself and so I choose not to do homework.

I infer from this statement and the remarks of two other seniors that some students find a balance between the school demands and their sense of self. The result is that they study—that is, read books that are unassigned or join a club that is not required.

WHERE AND WHEN TO STUDY AND DO HOMEWORK

The GI environment constrains studying. A student's academic schedule, the official school calendar, the residential rules and customs shape the time that is free and the locations that are open. Subject matter and the nature of an assignment are an important variable as to when to study.

Students may do homework or study at any time of the day, night, or weekend. To understand studying routines, remember the section on "Rhythms of the Day." The official schedule makes Sunday, Tuesday, and Thursday intense homework and study days. Mandatory study session from 6:30–8:00 p.m. is study time. I estimate that about half of the mandated study time was spent studying, 6:30–8:00 on Monday through Thursday, and the number of people actually in the study session is about 85% of the student body. A reliable estimate is tricky because of numerous exceptions. Students with the concurrence of the residence staff and the school guidance counselor are given exemptions to leave or "postpone" study session for music lessons, tutoring, sports team practices, rehearsals, and so forth.

After the study session ends, many continue studying, more or less. Other students leave their rooms to avoid homework by roaming the dorm or leaving the building. By 10:00 and 10:30 juniors and seniors, respectively, must return to the dorm. Then, until 12:30 students choose to do homework, to study, or to socialize. Many study sporadically during this period. Studying occurs in the dorm room alone or with friends in the study lounge. Some continue to "screw around" until 12:30 when serious homework begins, a characteristic of the boys' dorm according to both girls and boys.

During the day between classes, students are usually in their rooms doing homework or sleeping. If they study, it is usually solitary.

Reading is a sizable part of the total homework load. Some students, in order to find time to read during the day, choose to leave big blocks of time; others read when they can, here and there. One junior read during 10-minute breaks between classes. "I have ideally an hour and fifty minutes during the day that I could read, not counting the time before I go to class." I encountered a junior male sneaking into the university student center in the afternoon to find a place to read, acknowledging that he was breaking a rule by being in that building. I saw students sitting under a tree reading in the early afternoon. Students also race in and out of the computer lab finishing assignments and checking e-mail.

Students report that the practice of doing homework in class for another class rarely happens at GI; this is one way in which GI is different than other schools. Teachers and teaching fellows who have taught in typical high schools notice that, too. The only instance I saw of last-minute completion of homework was in a televised course with no instructor for a subsequent class.

Much studying occurs at night. Many students "stay up late" in order to finish their work. Some go to bed whether they are finished or not; some stay up until they are finished; and others stay up until they fall asleep. Boys are much more likely to stay up after 2:00 a.m. to do homework than are girls. Students talk about pulling all-nighters. Responses on a questionnaire where students were asked to estimate the number that they "pull" ranged from 0 to 25 per year. Discerning what constituted the properties of an all-nighter was never clear. I heard descriptions that sounded like getting sleep in the early morning was one of the attributes of the definition. I also woke up systematically to count lights in dorm windows over several nights to see how many people were up. Of course, having a light on in the middle of the night does not mean someone is studying. In other words, my observations and student statements about frequency did not match. Some of the gender differences may be associated with expressions of bravado and resistance to the rules in the structured GI environment, a topic I discuss in Chapter 6.

Girls do not go to other floors to fool around like boys do, according to senior girls; rather, they go to do homework. Many girls have homework done by 11:00 or 12:00 when many boys are just starting. The fourth floor of the boy's dorm took pride in claiming they did not start studying until 12:30. At the same time I intuitively detected a kind of subtle pressure, especially among the boys, to postpone studying until later in the night that some students have trouble resisting, although nothing was said about this overtly in interviews.

Solitary studying happens frequently, usually in a student's room, during the week. Some students study by themselves in order to keep up; others simply find it more efficient. A small number who have no roommate prefer the isolation for that reason. An interesting question is, What is the proportion of solitary studying to social studying? I neglected to think of this question in the field, so I have no confidence making an estimate.

Weekends are another time to study. Catching up on work that requires a large block of time is the goal of weekend studying. Sunday evening studying, which students place as part of the week, is not part of weekend studying. At the end of one math class, students were saying, "This is going to be a math weekend." A few students go home to study, claiming that their parents insist on it. Many students do not study until Sunday night. I suspect that more than doing homework is going on. One senior girl said the weekend was the "only time" she studied because she was "too busy the rest of the time." Another senior said she studied one night per weekend. Both of these people were successful GIites by anyone's definition and neither appeared particularly stressed by the pace of GI life. The boundaries between sleeping, eating, socializing, and studying on weekends are too fuzzy to classify activities unambiguously. For example, in October my field notes show one boy studying in the lounge on a Sunday morning while the rest of the dorm seems to be sleeping. A junior boy, later on the same day, woke up at 2:30 p.m. and described the day as, "Just spending my day in the room [his roommate has gone home]. I do this every day. I do not like the lounge downstairs and have a lot of homework."

TYPES OF HOMEWORK AND SUBJECT MATTER

Time and place influence patterns of studying and homework behavior, but are not the sole determiners. Examples of other considerations are the announcement of a test, the relationship with a teacher, the subject matter, and the kind of homework. The latter two are interwoven and are very important in the story of academic life at the Greenhouse Institute.

Four months into living at the Greenhouse Institute, a deeper story about homework emerged as I tried to understand the incongruity between study behavior and expression of self-identity in the form of "I am a science person," "I am a humanities person," and so forth. I mistakenly assumed that a person who identified with a subject area, such as science, would treat the homework in that domain in a thoughtful, careful way. Instead, I saw repeated instances in which the homework was done in a rote, thoughtless way. The key to understanding this situation was the classification of homework and the pace of GI life.

Students have a coherent system of classifying homework types. Interviewed students named from three to eight types, with the norm being four types. "Busywork" is the type of homework in which the expectation is to produce a set of facts. "Writing" homework is when the expectation is to craft a paper of specific length on a topic of varying complexity. "Reading" assignment is when the outcome is to be prepared to discuss a large number of pages. "Projects," the fourth type, are when the students are expected to synthesize information and present it often in a nonwritten format. Searching for variations based on gender, ethnicity, and time in program (juniors or seniors), and perceived success in the program revealed no apparent differences.

Student approach to homework varies in terms of a curriculum area and the way homework is experienced in associated courses. Science and math courses require primarily busywork homework. Humanities require reading homework.

Math homework is busywork. Therefore, it is attended to in short bursts of time when time is limited or in a social situation where one can easily switch attention to an ongoing conversation. Much science homework has that same feature, as do computer applications and languages. When the homework switches to labs in science and language, writing is required. That kind of homework is done on Tuesdays and Thursdays. Humanities are loaded with reading homework requiring a larger block of time, often time alone, and time for thinking. Humanities subjects homework is done either after other homework or on days when time is available during the day. This homework also tends to be done later at night. Clearly students are making choices about studying and doing homework.

Studying and socializing are commonly combined. Busywork is the kind of homework that predominates because students may finish quickly, be interrupted while studying, and suspend deep thinking in order to get the homework done. One example is a couple in a coffee shop silently doing homework. Another was when I participated with three male students in a role-playing game in which they did homework when waiting for a turn. A third is three female peers sporadically doing homework while discussing classes and boys and requesting music from a DJ on a local radio station in a dorm room.

TIME FREE FROM STUDYING

Looking or expecting a time to appear when homework and studying is completely done is unlikely at GI. Time is rarely free of homework because studying and homework are never really finished. Until the last exam, more assignments wait to be completed. So to say homework is done or to ask, as I did, "What do you do after homework and studying is done?" is to get a collection of incomprehensible answers. Being done with homework is really an arbitrary point determined by the student. When a student says "I am done with an assignment" or "I have done what is due for tomorrow," it is meant in the narrowest sense. Many students report they never feel they are finished. One student remarked that in the whole year she might have had a 2-week stint when her homework was done.

FOUR MODES OF ADJUSTMENT TO HOMEWORK

Knowing the general pattern of studying is an incomplete description of how students actually do it. Four modes of adjustment to the press of homework emerged. Using the students mentioned in Chapter 3 as examples, the patterns are: Tracie—taking-it-in-stride, or striders; Wanda—defending on the edge, or defenders; Marvin—socializing over academics; and Samir—doing the right thing, or struggler.

The study patterns of individuals within each general pattern are shaped by the student's vision of future self, "the person I could be in the future." Thoughts of one's future are common at GI because students come there to get ready for the next place, usually college. Their orientation to the future takes two contrasting forms. One form is "goal-directed" toward some known end point, such as a career or a specific college; the other form I call "unfinished" because the orientation is toward an unknown, ill-defined future. These contrasting notions of self differentiate among students and influence how they handle the academic demands.

I construct voices of students to illustrate the way in which homework is interpreted by students and how they would describe themselves. The voices are my construction of multiple students. Beside each name I provide two labels. The first designates the orientation to the future; the second, the general study pattern.

Strugglers

The first pattern of adjustment to GI life that I want to look at is that of the strugglers. These are students who struggle mightily to meet the demands of the institution and part of their struggle is generated by their own way of perceiving the situation. The best example of this group is Samir. I found no examples of unfinished orientation and struggling as I define it.

Samir's pattern was "doing the right thing" and "struggling to do it" because of his often expressed allegiance to his family's traditional values. Samir, a junior, drove himself to do all the work and would push until he was exhausted, even though he did not believe you could do all the homework the way he wanted. This occurred in a cyclical pattern. Among the four, only he studied consistently during study session. Samir was organized about his studying as well as his social life. He had good study and time management skills, but his values prevented him from setting priorities that would enable him to experience less pressure. Samir generally maintained a very positive attitude toward the school despite the pressure, was motivated to learn as much as he could, and was reconciled that time and the amount of work required meant that he could not study the way he would have preferred. My guess is that Samir will modify his approach as a senior and become a strider.

Samir (goal-directed, struggler) would say the following about homework: "There is not enough time to get it done the way I would like according to my family's values. I cannot do it halfway when I do it. So I keep trying to do it all."

Socializers

Marvin's operating principle about doing homework is "socializing over academics." Unless he has no choice, he is going to choose social activity and postpone academic demands. Marvin is a realist in that he does what needs to get done. His relaxed, confident style keeps him from being overwhelmed by the demands. He recognizes that feeling overloaded is a result of his procrastination. Marvin does not think all the work can be done and he does not try to do it. His lack of concern for grades and accomplishment moderates his tension. Marvin will do the work, yet he does not seem to push himself to new heights. He claims he loves to learn, but is satisfied with getting the main idea and not obsessed with the details and thus for him, grades. Most of his studying is done in a social situation with friends. My guess is that Marvin is going to handle it the way he does even when he is a senior. I have separated Marvin from the other modes to highlight the desire for socialization in many students. In reality, socialization must combine with the other three modes for a student to remain at GI.

Marvin (goal-directed, socializer) would say the following about homework: "There is enough time, but you cannot get it all done and socialize. Still, you can get by okay."

Defenders

A third characteristic pattern of adjustment to the homework demands of GI is that of the defenders. These students arrived with excitement, encountered the demands, and began to wonder if they should really be at GI.

Wanda is active in "defending" her place at GI as she hangs "on the edge" of imminent disaster. She is caught in a pattern that offers sporadic relief from the press of homework; yet she is pulled toward spending time socializing, which impinges on the time she should be studying. Entering GI, Wanda was worried about getting the work done. She has learned to deal with the situation, but she still cannot relax because she has persistent doubts of being able to fit in academically. Wanda seems unable to reconcile herself to GI. Wanda separates the school part from the dorm part of the institute. Of the four, Wanda has the weakest study skills and a less realistic view of the school. Luck also may have been unkind to her and increased the academic and social pressure she feels. Wanda has a class schedule that places her in class at times when others study, and she has teachers who have styles of teaching that reinforce Wanda's poor study decisions. Her adjustment is made more difficult by chance factors. My guess is that Wanda's turmoil will continue. She will remain on the defensive as she struggles with the academic demands and with her personal conflict about staying. Her adventurous spirit might keep her going. I expected her not to return as a senior, but when I return for a visit for a member check, she greeted me warmly.

Wanda (goal-directed, defender) would say the following about homework: "There is not enough time. I can barely keep up. I have learned to get by doing what is required."

Dan (unfinished orientation, defender) would say the following about homework: "There is enough time. I do not want to do it. You can get past the requirements because they do not want to send you home."

Take-it-in-Striders

Tracie's approach to doing homework follows the majority pattern of "taking-it-in-stride." She experiences the intensity of GI in an apparently less stressful way than many of her classmates. Recognizing that homework is something that needs to be done, Tracie organizes her time to do it. There is enough time to get most work done. She worries and has feelings of being overloaded; yet those thoughts lead toward resolution. Needing more time, she requests it and uses the resources of GI to her advantage. Tracie does not let the homework requirement push her beyond her limits or her sense of self. When she is tired, she goes to sleep. Tracie is committed to learning and makes time to read what interests her outside of homework assignments. In her view, inappropriate school rules encourage irresponsible behavior and lead her peers to use teachers as scapegoats. Tracie loves GI, seems to extract what it has to offer, and is ready to move on to another experience. Tracie seems to be in the right place. The take-it-in-stride group, or the striders, are the majority within the Greenhouse Institute. The group has several variations in study patterns.

Tracie (goal-directed, strider) would say the following about homework: "There is enough time. I get done what needs to be done and get more time, if I need it."

Pat (goal-directed, strider) would say the following about homework: "There is enough time, if you do not slack off. Sometimes, I do not do everything, but mostly I do. It will come together by the time of the test."

Willard (unfinished orientation, strider) would say the following about homework: "There is enough time, but I do not want to do it, unless it is helping me to grow."

Chip (unfinished orientation, strider) would say the following about homework: "There is enough time, but I do not care much, unless I am interested."

George (unfinished orientation, strider) would say about homework: "There is enough time. I keep up by doing what is necessary and I want to have social relationships."

Comparing the four cases, Tracie's story is the most common. She takes GI in stride by experiencing the intensity, having occasional misgivings, and looking toward the future. In my list of 89 people with whom I spoke periodically at GI, the majority are in this group. Taking it in stride fits more seniors than juniors. A strong possibility is that Tracie might have arrived with the propensity to behave in the manner in which she did. Among the three juniors, I found signs of their characteristic pattern of adjustment in my early field notes about them. However, the signs are not so strong as to convince me that the context of GI is not the prime influence on adjustment.

INDIVIDUALS ADJUST TO PERCEIVED HOMEWORK OVERLOAD

I was haunted by the thought, How is it that some students handle the GI situation so well and others do not? Why is it that students like Samir and Wanda are experiencing more stress than Tracie and Marvin? Can I make sense of the variation? The homework demands are significant, but students with apparently comparable ability and interests respond differently. The basis of individual adjustment to homework demands is the answer to two questions: Is there enough time to get the work done, and What does this homework have to do with who I am?

When students feel overwhelmed by the homework demands, they feel "overloaded," a point when the homework demands exceed the time available to complete assignments. Feeling overloaded means one must evaluate the situation and decide if they have enough time to complete the assignments. The four kinds of homework, mentioned earlier, were replete with reference to time, too. The judgment of "enough time" is not obvious. All students experience overload, but what looks like it to an observer may not be interpreted by a student as such. Many students believe that there is generally enough time, but their procrastination brings on the overload. They blame themselves more than the institution. Interestingly, during "hell weeks," or midterm and final exam periods, the amount of hysteria did not seem particularly heavy. Residential counselors and many students would not agree with my observation.

If overload is in the eye of the beholder, what perceptual elements are shaping the experience for students? Perceptions of time and of self are key. Neither time nor self are constants, psychologically speaking. Under varying conditions and interpretations, time can seem to move rapidly or slowly. In the former, one is concentrating or focused on the task at hand; in the latter, one is disorganized and grasping for solutions to get to the end of the situation. How one interprets feeling overloaded is important for understanding individual reaction. One's sense of self (or selves) is related to study practices noted earlier in the chapter—that is, when I described students differentiating between homework and studying the notion of self emerged in the statement "Homework I do for school, studying I do for me." Other notions of students' selves appear throughout the data. Students often refer to themselves as a math person, an early morning person, a medical person. Once stated, students said nothing more by way of explanation in the conversation, as if the declaration's obvious implications conveyed all the meaning about them. In other words, defining one's self explains one's behavior. We saw hints of this relationship in the homework patterns of Tracie—taking-it-in-stride, or striders; Wanda—defending on the edge, or defenders; Marvin—socializing over academics, or socializing; and Samir—doing the right thing, or struggler.

When two students of apparently comparable ability and similar coursework are having wildly different experiences, the power of personal perception about self and overload is revealed.

The voices of students presented earlier illustrate the four patterns of adjustment to the academic demands of the school. The students' orientation to the future and their orientation to themselves seem to modify how they handle the situation of overload. The majority of students in the strider category have moments of discomfort and anxiety when they are overwhelmed, but basically they believe they can get it done, and they do. Interestingly, some striders—namely, the goal-directed group—know where they are going, while those in the unfinished group are successfully moving through the Greenhouse Institute, too, albeit less engaged in the academics. The number of students who fit the second pattern, the socializers, is elusive because these students are successful at navigating the school and most become striders as they become seniors. The third pattern is that of the strugglers, which is a small group. I presented one example, Samir, of the three I identified. Note how the struggler is caught by his own belief structure, which places him in jeopardy in the GI community. The last group, the defenders, is small, too. These people probably have the basic ability to do the work, find it not engaging, and choose to grit it out rather than leave. My guess is that they choose to stay because the home and local school environment is less attractive than the Greenhouse Institute.

STUDENTS' REGARD FOR CLASSES

Doing homework is not the complete GI academic experience. It dominates students' lives, but homework originates in classes. What is it like to be in a class at an academically rigorous school? How do students judge their classes and teacher? These are important questions because many chose to attend GI for the advanced challenging classes and little is known about what it is like to be in such classes.

Overall, students are happy with their teachers and their classes. Juniors are enthusiastic about the quality of the teaching, their peers, and the challenging nature of the classes. A junior female exclaimed, "The classes are vivacious." Seniors believe they are getting a strong preparation for college. The curriculum is divided into two broad divisions: science/math and humanities. Physics, Calculus, Chemistry, Computer Applications, Literature, Chinese, French, British Literature, Lost Generation Poets, and Civilization are all examples of courses offered at GI.

While GI has a highly qualified teaching staff, variation among teachers is obvious. Students have varying opinions about classes and teachers, and even of the same class. A student may love the class, while some peers do not. In a joint interview with two girls, one remarked how she "hated" the math class and her friend said it was her "favorite class."

The key concepts in understanding how students think of classes are content, interest, and the teacher. These variables, in turn, are modified by terms such as *challenging, amount of work,* and *ability.*

"Ordinary" classes are those that are routine, not exciting, "comfortable," and in which the teacher does not seem involved, either. The amount of work is reasonable. The class and the teachers go in a "steady, expected" pattern, which can occur in science, history, language, computer classes, and even Advanced Placement (AP) and non-AP classes. Interaction between teacher and students is limited. The low interest of a student in the subject matter often makes the difference in placing a class inside the ordinary category. Are many classes deemed ordinary? Determining the proportion was slippery. Students were hesitant to make estimates acknowledging the diversity of courses and teachers. The struggling students seemed to find it easier to make such statements, but on the whole no estimates were trustworthy. For a while I thought it had to do primarily with interest, but that is not enough. A student might not have much interest in a subject, yet it becomes interesting, not ordinary due to the teacher. So a class might escape being classified as "ordinary" when the teacher is seen as caring and interested.

Favorite classes, as might be expected, had characteristics that were opposite those of ordinary and least favorite classes. The term *favorite* was applied to courses throughout the curriculum using the variables of content, interest, and teachers, too. A "cool teacher" was the most important variable. Students like courses that fit within their personal interest and ability—for example, humanities people like classes in that particular curricular area. Favorite classes are challenging, interesting because of one's interest or the teacher's ability to make it interesting, and quite interactive. These qualities enable students to override the pull of tiredness and approaching deadlines.

Two unsettling observations emerged in my search to understand the meaning of favorite courses. The first, which I observed frequently, was that students expressed puzzlement when they realized that their favorite course was not in their self-defined ability. For example, Japanese was a favorite over Chemistry. The use of the discussion method by a skilled teacher was what was attractive, although a discussion was not used exclusively in those classes. The second observation was that one favorite course was outside the regular courses and occurred during a special 2-week term in May before graduation.

Categorizing a class as "least favorite" is closely linked to the teacher. "He doesn't teach like anyone learns" was a strong negative comment. In those cases routine replaces any real teaching. A student might say, "He just spat out information, we wrote it down, and did homework." Curriculum content was not important to being designated least favorite. Difficulty and perceived relevance of content influenced some evaluations. One kind of course, televised courses that were beamed around the state, was singled out more for mention than others.

INSIDE CLASSROOMS IN VARIOUS SUBJECTS

What actually happens in classes in schools like the Greenhouse Institute is not generally known. Are classes similar to those at any high school, from the student perspective? That question cannot be answered by this section. The purpose of this section is to provide a peek into classes for those who might consider going to the Greenhouse Institute, and for those who wonder how different might they be. I leave that judgment to the reader.

In such a small environment, describing classes and mentioning the content specifically could be linked to individual teachers. To avoid any hint of evaluation, I combine elements from classes of a given type.

The individuality among teachers is evident. At the same time, curriculum areas, like science and humanities, have classes that group into characteristic patterns. I do not know how much of the pattern is the subject matter, the custom within the curriculum area, or the personality of the teachers. The experience of taking any class obviously varies because of the student (in terms of interest and preparation), the composition of the class, the teachers (in terms of teaching style, experience teaching the course, and prior teaching experience) and the curriculum.

Humanities Classes

In humanities classes (literature, history, languages), students must read large amounts of text. Discussion is the most frequently used method of instruction. Many classes are arranged in a circle, or more conversationally encouraging configuration. Lecture is often interspersed with recitation and discussion.

In the following paragraphs, I describe a literature class, in order to illustrate classes in the humanities area. Besides participation in discussion, which is often graded, students produce projects or papers and take tests to demonstrate what they have learned.

The 1:00 class is in a nondescript classroom with 16 desks in a square. Most arrive after having had three or four earlier classes. Lighthearted bantering occurs among the students. The teacher starts immediately by quoting from the reading and drawing their attention to important terms. The level of response is not acceptable. "Why didn't you look this up before class?" he asks rhetorically. A girl responds, "I did not think the words were that important." The teacher simply states "You need to look 'presentment' [and other terms you do not know] up and connect it to the text." The teacher directs the class to the second paragraph. Students volunteer answers, such as "I like the metaphor." The teacher follows up comments by asking about the symbolism: "Our biblical scholars help us out on this one." The students offer explanations. The teacher uses one student comment to extend the conversation to another student, repeatedly asking for examples from the reading that support points. The teacher compliments students after responses and urges them to go deeper. The teacher lectures briefly about some points. The teacher does not supply the correct answer. Typical phrases are "that is pretty good . . . other thoughts?" "Decent conjecture . . . ." "How do you explain this in terms of the reading about . . . ?" "Follow that line of thinking . . . ." "I am not saying you are in error . . . ." Fifteen of the 16 students are involved to varying degrees. Going forward without pausing, the teacher states, "You argued an earlier paper about heroism, I wonder can you make a connection between heroism and the text." A student pinpoints a selection and reads to illustrate her thinking.

Papers are returned. "Good writing parallels good thinking," the teacher reminds them. Students ask questions. The teacher invites them to talk to him now in class or in his office before the next paper is due. "If there are no questions for the general group, go, or set up an appointment." Class ends.

Science Classes

Science classes are predominantly recitations and lectures mixed with demonstrations, some problem solving, and preparation for the labs, which meet on a fourth day, a characteristic of science classes and language classes. Evaluation is primarily through tests, although homework assignments might be graded. Preparation for Advanced Placement tests is in everyone's minds. The classes have numerous instances of "tips" on how to interpret a test question or do something relevant to the exam. The classes move quickly and are filled with facts and formulas. The classes tend to be in lab rooms with high tables and uncomfortable stool-like chairs. The example in the following paragraphs exemplifies a typical GI science class.

The class has 14 students—half are girls, half are minorities—sitting with their notebooks open and their calculators by their sides. The class starts with a quick review of a trial AP exam question they did for homework. "If you got less than fifteen, start focusing now."

A student interjects, "Are we doing fun stuff today?" The teacher smiles and keeps going. The class is a repeating series of segments: tell/demonstrate/you-do-it/we-do-it-together/student's questions are solicited. The chemical structure of DNA is the topic. Using the TV camera and diagrams, associated questions are flashed before the class. The teacher moves back and forth between earlier learning, either in this class or in biology or chemistry, to draw the students into the topic. The teacher pointedly states: "This is a tip." Activity changes quickly from the white board to the VCR to a demonstration. The students act out the DNA chain. Questions are usually geared to recall of facts, principles, or some application. Often, if there is no response, the answer is supplied. As class ends, the teacher points to the assignment on the blackboard. "Think, practice, folks," he says in farewell. Students ask no questions about future assignments.

Mathematics Classes

I highlight two math classes in order to illustrate a subtle difference in the student body—those who are educationally malnourished and those who have been educationally enriched. Placement in mathematics classes is determined by a standardized test. Classes in mathematics have cyclical patterns that are similar to those of science classes. The basic format is: the teacher reviews homework problems, the teacher presents a new problem, the teacher answers questions, students do it, the class reviews the answers, then there are more questions, and the cycle repeats. Performance on Advanced Placement tests is in the minds of students and faculty, too. The difference between the advanced math classes and the other classes is readily observable in terms of student behavior.

Math and Educational Malnourishment. Lack of enriched math teaching and lack of opportunity for algebra places students in this class. The class has an opportunity to alter a student's perception of competence in math. Sixteen students sit at desks in three rows with white boards on the walls and a calculator, which is hooked into an overhead projector.

The teacher speaks as follows about the homework: "If it is satisfactory to you, turn it in." In response to a request, the teacher negotiates an extension of time until 4:00 of that day. Next week's test is described: "Yes, memorize the equations, but having a calculator is okay and it has a memory so you can have stuff in it, but you will have to figure out how to get it in." The class suggests homework problems to review.

One girl exclaims, "I got it!" The teacher looks at it and says, "It is correct." She beams with such happiness that he gives her a high five. One of her girlfriends jumps up and gives her one, too. She states, "I only used common sense, not a fancy formula, to figure it out!" (I interpreted her excitement to be a sign that she became aware that math could be common sense and she could do it. Later, the teacher agrees, smiling.)

A boy asks, "Where would cubic functions come up in life?" The teacher responds: "Good question. We will see a film showing how math fits into life. Building boat hulls and quadratic equations are useful in a number of ways." Listening, a girl volunteers to her male classmate, "I have never seen a video on math!" He responds, "that is what makes the school different."

Math in an Advanced Class. Enriched prior experience pays off and tacit knowledge about the AP test is evident. The class has nine students, mostly seniors, of which two are girls. The teacher passes out tests advising them that they will receive an e-mail describing their mistakes on their papers. "Accuracy, precision, and presentation" are keys to a major assignment. The teacher continues, "No open book on the AP test, but you can have a calculator, so put in whatever you need to know. Today, we will spend half our time on homework problems." The teacher gives tips on how the questions would look on the AP exam.

Groups are formed to compare calculations. Four students are in front scrutinizing what one has done. A student says, "What happened, I do not understand?" Another student shows her. The group is so focused on the problem that they do not hear the teacher asking the whole class for an explanation of problem number 62. The teacher interjects into the group, "She proved it in reverse. It is correct, but on the exam it would be wrong because that is not what they asked." Complete silence follows as the teacher works the problem. "Who wants me to continue?" Several shake their head no. The teacher stops. (Later, the teacher explains, "Once they understand, typically they do not want to continue.")

A student explains problem number 62, a series of graphs. The teacher tells them to go deeper: "Explain how and why you did [what you did]. Problems like this will always be on the test." The teacher compliments students: "Hey, the calculator does not know that entering that value is impossible, it just does what you want. Be careful. You have to interpret." A student remarks, "Be smarter than the calculator."

Classes Specific to This School

The Greenhouse Institute curriculum contains a variety of courses, many not typically offered in the standard comprehensive high school. They are colloquia, independent study, and research courses. The courses enable students to learn techniques and engage in various forms of inquiry. The colloquia courses are like seminars and demand that students synthesize and apply information and provide a unique flavor to the academic stew. Below is an example of a typical colloquium.

A Senior Colloquium. One hundred plus seniors are jammed into the boys' lounge on couches, floor, tables, and chairs. Some lean against the walls or stand in the doorways. Five students play the roles of famous scientists from various periods in history with differing visions in a meeting as they respond to questions and to each other. Students, male and female, assume the roles (Copernicus, Galileo, Bohr, Sagan, Einstein) affecting appropriate dress and accents. The subject matter is serious, but there is room for fun, too. When Einstein, trying to illustrate the meaning of relativity, asks Carl Sagan, "Please explain the notion of time by sitting on a hot stove or sitting on a hot woman," there is absolute silence and an explosion of laughter. Some students ask questions of the panel. The conversation segues into a video of a scientist, politician, and poet. The teacher ends with a quote for them to consider: "Only by fusing science and humanities can we progress. . . ."

CLUB TIME IS PART OF ACADEMICS

The final piece of academic life is the presence of clubs, which are small collections of students who share a common interest. The Greenhouse Institute hosts a wide variety of clubs. The clubs represent the varied interests of the students and of the faculty. Students join them ostensibly to make their college applications read better, but my observations suggest more than casual involvement for many. Some clubs are connected to courses such as the language classes or the Astronomy Club. These clubs enrich the academic content of courses. Some represent the ethnic diversity of the school and their mission is to help others understand them. Examples are the Afro-American Club, Persian Club, and Indian Club. These clubs increase contact among students and broaden their understanding of diversity. The Japanese Club is a language-related club and an ethnic-related club. Some clubs are connected to hobbies and to sports, such as the "Walleyball" Club (a comic derivative of volleyball), Chess Club, Choir, and Music Club. Two clubs stood out for me as being unusual and suggest further the role a club can have. One was the Institute Students for Radical Change (of GI), and the other was the Institute Sexual Orientation Support Group (for students to understand and communicate about sexual orientation). Both clubs exemplify the institution's responsiveness to the needs of the student body. Some of the clubs are very active and others exist more in name. Usually the membership roster is larger than is represented by those who are regularly active in the club. A good example was the African-American Club, which had 60 members, but I saw no more than 10 Black and White students at any meeting. They conducted activities like Soul Food Night, a dance, and a Habitat for Humanity project. Interestingly, there was neither a computer club nor a rock/alternate music club.

CONCLUSION

Academic Life is a pillar of the GI experience. Students choose GI for the rigorous academics, and they find more than they anticipated. They must adapt to the swiftly moving content; the demanding homework assignments; the knowledgeable and challenging teachers; and the fast-learning, serious peers. They are excited, engaged, and overwhelmed at times.

Much of non–class time is spent in academically oriented activities such as studying, going to the library, reading, and club membership. Students learn to study and manage their time. Some learn to study for the first time; others regain a love of learning. Students create a taxonomy of kinds of homework. Students study differently depending on subject and kind of homework in response to their perception of the demands. Most students feel overloaded at some point. Students' responses to studying fall into the following categories: those who take it in stride, those who struggle, and those who defend. Adjustment to academic demand is related to notions of self.

The life in classrooms at GI is familiar yet subtly different. When students who want to learn meet teachers who are knowledgeable about the content, the change in level of discussion and quality of interactions is apparent. However, these serious students behave like the American adolescents they are. Being serious does not mean they do not act up, goof off, and refrain from expressing opinions about classes and teachers.

Classes at GI are different from those at local high schools, according to the students. Science and math classes follow a pattern that differs from humanities classes. The content, personal interest, and teacher influence whether a course is ordinary or a favorite. Teachers are very important. Mixing students who are serious about learning with teachers who love their content leads to an exciting academic experience.

CHAPTER FIVE

Living in the Dorm

Academics are only half of the Greenhouse Institute experience; the other 60% is residential. My mathematics emphasizes that being away from home is more than going to school. The residential life component of the Greenhouse Institute has a profound effect on students. Students leave the familiarity of their homes and enter a complex world where they may become the person they aspire to be. Students encounter situations that are unlike home in that they are less personal, more institutional, and more circumscribed. Students, commenting on what it is like to be at GI, make more references to residential than academic life. All see GI as confining. The statement, "being at GI is like a minimum-security prison," mentioned earlier, captures the experience of many. Others liken it to "going to camp," only with more restrictions.

Students find that living in the dorm offers challenges. Just as the rigorous academics caught them unprepared, so does residential life. The rhythms of the Greenhouse Institute are played out in the arena of residential life just as powerfully as that of academic life. Embedded in RL are requirements that are not strictly academic, but which are part of the graduation requirements nonetheless.

Living in the dorm is a major adjustment for students. Dorm life means proximity with strangers. The physical space is new. The institutional surroundings are simply not particularly inviting. Half of one's peers (the seniors) are familiar with the rules, already know each other, and have a network of social relationships. A system of rules is in place that these strangers explain. Adults tell students that the rules are for their safety and that a support structure is there should they have problems adjusting. It is assumed that the person living in the dorm will be responsible and make good choices.

RESIDENTIAL LIFE IS AND IS NOT A HOME

During their first few months, students describe GI as "going away to school." For new students, home is where your family and local school are. While all students return home over long weekend holidays called "extendeds," and for major holidays such as Thanksgiving and Christmas, some students choose to return home every weekend. Eventually, most students begin to regard the Greenhouse Institute as home, although it happens at different rates. This marks a significant point in their relationship to GI and to their parents. One student said it happened in the first month; another, not until November. One junior explains for many others,

> Whenever I'm at home now, it like doesn't feel like home anymore. I mean, a lot of people here haven't adopted the institute as their home yet, they don't accept the institute as their home like I do. You know, this is definitely my home rather than just the place where I live. And so like, when I go home, I feel awkward, like a visitor. [Larry: When did you realize that happened to you?] Um . . . I think it was probably . . . maybe the second extended weekend. 'Cause I mean there was the first one and then there was a whole month. [Larry: There was the August, and then the September one?] So, the second weekend I was like you know, I really just don't belong in this house anymore. Because I'm so much more comfortable and I feel like . . . maybe not accepted, except like, I have more motivation to be accepted at GI. [Larry: You mean you want to be accepted here?] Yeah. I mean not really by people though, I mean basically just by the environment. Like you know, I want this to be my home. Whereas like at home you know, I don't really care 'cause I'm only going to be there like once a month.

This quote exemplifies significant elements of student thought. The feeling that one is home is accompanied by the belief that one can behave without worrying about acceptance. "You are never far from a friend here." The student realized that not all his peers have this feeling of home, yet his expectation is that it will happen to everyone as it has for him. Finally, GI is where basic needs like sleeping, eating, friendships, and personal attention are met and the most time is spent.

No student told me his or her family was happy with the news that GI had become home. Families were sad about being displaced, but rationalized that the child was happier. One student told his family, "I feel like I have no home to go to," a statement that made his mother cry and his father angry. It is confusing to parents that when their children say "GI is home," the children are actually saying the GI community is their home. Rarely are they disregarding their family. GI becomes home because one is embedded in a community where one belongs.

The Greenhouse Institute creates opposing feelings in young people. Students want to leave and hunger to come back. This is similar to feelings expressed by first-year college students. The meaning of GI as home is conflicted: it both is and is not a home. Strong negative emotions coexist with warm feelings in the students' minds.

The Greenhouse Institute is certainly not a conventional home. This fact is revealed to students in subtle and obvious ways. Their homes have characteristics that are not matched by the GI environment. In a traditional home, autonomy and trust grow between parent and child. Reliability and trustworthiness are rewarded by granting more autonomy. When children do something inappropriate parents may limit autonomy, but over time lost trust may be reclaimed. At GI, regaining lost autonomy and earning it back is very hard to do. Opportunities are available to show trustworthiness and to change inappropriate behavior, but gaining more autonomy is rarely the outcome. GI speaks of individuality, yet students are governed by rules for a group. Groupthink is familiar in a residential life staff meeting: "If we do that for [Sarah,] it will open a Pandora's Box, what will we say to the others?"

Homes also are characterized by general sharing of information among family members. Privacy exists, yet family members often know what the others are doing. But at GI students are routinely told, "I cannot talk about that." Residential Counselors (RC) withhold information from each other and they teach their residential assistants this principle. In general, information is privileged. Students are left to accept statements about why things happen, such as sanctions against student behavior, with no explanation. Misinterpretations and resentment builds. One RC commenting on the conflict between maintaining confidentiality in the face of student inquiry, wanting to share, and the dictum of confidentiality, said, "You have to throw yourself on your sword."

Other characteristics of GI life that are inconsistent with typical family life are the constancy of family membership and the treatment of illness. Typically, membership in homes remains stable over lengthy periods. Family members rarely urge other members to leave (withdraw). At home, brothers and sisters who misbehave are not sent away. Furthermore, half the family does not leave each year (graduation). The way in which illness is handled at GI is also unlike the way families act. When a child becomes sick and verbally expresses it, that state is accepted as real. At GI, however, saying one is sick is likely to fall on unreceptive ears: the nurse questions it with a skeptical tone in her voice and suspects illness is being used as an excuse for not doing work. These characteristics of the Greenhouse Institute conflict with home life. They remind students that RL is both a home and is not a home.

LIKE A MINIMUM-SECURITY PRISON

What compels students to say, "Being at GI is like a minimum-security prison?" It is a reaction to an adult world that places definite boundaries on adolescent behavior. Parents send their children to GI on a university campus for the academics and expect a safe environment. The Greenhouse Institute assures parents that supervision is everywhere; but students see just a bunch of rules. At Orientation the student and family sign a statement honoring the rules.

How do students rationalize why there are rules? For the most part, students share the adult view that the rules are for the students' protection. "Some [of the rules] are reasonable because we're away from home, we're still considered minors for the most part," said a junior. Recognizing danger in the world is another reason for the curfew rule and the two-person rule of signing out with a peer. Students combine two ideas as a third rationale for having rules. Attending GI is "a privilege and they allow us to live here." Closely allied is the idea of being a guest in a home where one adheres to the house's rules. Few openly welcome rules as a means for protecting them from themselves. A junior, Cindy, offered that the rules enabled her to "build a pattern" to regulate her behavior. She does not like the rules; rather, she sees them as having a function. Accepting the notion that rules are for your protection does not mean that students accept them. Many students say there are too many rules and restrictions and discount them. In their view, the rules teach students to be immature and irresponsible. Students prefer a laissez-faire policy of enforcement: If a student cannot handle the GI experience, then the student should go home. "Why should we have all these rules for the small percent that cannot handle the situation?" One student captured much of his peers' thinking:

> Like if you're mature enough to stay out to like two in the morning
> because you like the nighttime better, and, you know, you're outside
> doing your work, which I think is perfectly fine, too. I don't know
> why we have to be in the building, but except, everybody knows that
> parents would go nuts if everybody had a two o'clock building curfew.

Most students accept that coming to GI means giving up freedom they had at home. The most lamented loss is mobility, because students cannot have cars. The students believe the rules exist to confine their natural activity and rights. While they recognize the protective nature of the rules, they favor independence over protection. The rules to keep track of where and what the students are doing are the most offensive and restrictive: check-in, leaving in pairs, study hours, no smoking, and curfew. Four of the rules, excluding smoking, have the effect of curtailing opportunities for "making bad choices," which is GI talk for breaking the rules. Check-in occurs in the later afternoon, and also before study hours. Check-in generally means "your RC should see you." Leaving in pairs has obvious implications for safety and it reduces lone individuals from engaging in solitary, perhaps dangerous, activity, since one has to find another person in order to sign out. The few dating couples find this a blessing. Study hours require students to spend one and a half hours in their rooms from 6:30–8:00 p.m. so they do some studying. Curfew refers to being back in the dorm by a set time. The curfew is set at a time that is much earlier than students want and later than some adults want. Nevertheless, the curfew limits opportunities to become involved in university party life because for collegians, heavy partying starts after GI students have to be back in the dorm.

The school continually frames discussion of the rules in terms of "We care about you" and "We want you to become an independent person who makes good choices." "There are a great number of people here who care about you. If residential counselors see you making a wrong choice, they will help you make better ones," the Residential Life director states. Even the school police officer makes enforcement personal: "My main concern is [your] safety . . . it would hurt me if something happened to you." The message is clear in official publications and throughout orientation day.

> The Greenhouse Institute is a holistic school where student choices have an affect on the entire academic experience and behavior in the residential aspect affects the academic aspect and vice versa. (Greenhouse Institute, 1996, p. 9)

Residential Life sees itself as the caregiving part of the school that recognizes the totality of students. RL asserts that student choice determines how one lives at GI, and their role is to help students make wise choices and acquire the skills necessary for a full life. RL invites students to participate in decision making but relinquishes no power to them.

The most common beliefs about rules among students were that rules are necessary, rules are enforced inconsistently, and rules teach irresponsibility. Rules also generate resistance. I found instances of most rules being stretched and bent, if not broken. I return to the meaning of this part of the story in Chapter 6.

ENFORCING RULES AND RESIDENCE COUNSELORS' ROLE

The Greenhouse Institute tries to have a humane policy that fits the state's law and the students' developmental needs. RL must deal with the range of culturally relevant and family relevant values and associated behaviors that the students bring to the school. The role of residence counselor is crucial. Residential counselors are advocates, disciplinarians, adult friends, and sometimes role models. "The kids come first" is the RC mantra. RCs must be sensitive enough to discern the needs and concerns of their students and distant enough to enforce rules and administer sanctions. RCs are the enforcers of the rules in most instances.

Students like their residence counselors. Seniors, more than juniors, regard their RC as a friend, a confidante, but not a parent. "I already have a parent." The relationship between an RC and students differs on each side of the dorm and seem gender-stereotypic. The tradition at GI is that RCs are generous with their time. Students expect them to be available all the time. Living in close proximity makes this possible. RCs find it conflicting not to be available. An RC, using a vampire metaphor, said, "The kids can suck you dry." Yet they do make themselves available even when they have time off.

Residential counselors do many little things that make GI a friendly place. For example, they maintain an open-door policy. Many RC rooms are organized to be inviting. Students can be found hanging out in them on many evenings watching videos, talking, and borrowing food from the refrigerator. For the quiet, asocial kind of students, RCs fill an important role. On numerous occasions, I found students who were generally invisible in the lounge and in the dining hall sitting, talking, and eating in a RC room. Some RCs make opportunities for social occasions such as birthday parties or recognition ceremonies for those who did something noteworthy.

Another aspect of the RC role that makes them indispensable for students is that RCs are responsible for transporting students on "runs" to restaurants, movies, stores, and so forth. In addition, as part of their official role, RCs conduct programs for students to earn Wellness credit for graduation. The Wellness program, which will be described in detail in Chapter 6, requires students participate in activities to round out their experience. The most compelling program I observed was "Coming Out Week," which was intended to help students, straight and gay, understand and deal with homosexuality in a constructive manner. Through discussions, role play, and listening to invited speakers, students learned to distinguish myths from facts and experienced prejudice. As a mark of solidarity with their gay peers, some students decided to dress in denim. This action bothered those students who did not know about the symbolism and either had or had not worn denim. Their gay peers expressed happiness at the support.

All is not smooth between Residence Counselors and the students. RCs often have to remind students of rules or homework, a task neither likes. Students want a laissez-faire policy. Two aspects of Residential Life generate the most heat: the enforcement of the rules and invasion of privacy, both which lead to a feeling of mistrust.

If RL has a rule, it is likely to be enforced. When a student breaks a major rule, they are "written up." Counselors interpret the wording of rules. Tension is created between blanket absolute enforcement and individualized context-related enforcement. This variance makes the students angry. "Inconsistent" was the term used by students to refer to enforcement. Complaints about inconsistency have a paradoxical quality because students want both uniform enforcement and attention to individual situations. Significantly, the inconsistency students decry keeps the environment humane and GI from becoming the "minimum-security prison" that some students claim it is.

Students recite multiple examples of inconsistency. The general meaning is that the RC is treating the same offense differently. They ignore the policy that counselors have discretion to interpret rules in a manner that fits their group. For example, two students are in a room filled with smoke. One is caught smoking and put into the three-tiered program to end smoking; the other is grounded. In another example, students who are judged not to be studying are grounded to their room to study from 8:00–9:30, while a student who is compulsively studying is ordered not to study for one evening.

Students question how adults can enforce rules at one time and not another. When in a public meeting students point out multiple well-known instances of rule-breaking, the adults retort that they are unaware of them and cannot operate on hearsay. Students are not going to report their peers, so the situation stays volatile. The students suspect some purposeful picking on certain individuals.

The second source of bad relationships has to do with students feeling mistrusted. The feeling is started by rules about leaving the building and the requirement that students sign in, and is amplified by the use of surveillance cameras in hallways. The feeling reaches a crescendo in the searches of rooms for illegal substances such as drugs and alcohol. Students express feelings of being violated. Adults are angry that some students use such substances. Every incident results in an imbalance in RL-student relationships for a period of weeks. Mistrust is rampant. Upon my return in February, everyone was grumbling about one incident. Several distressed-looking students shared thoughts of "getting out, leaving" because of their "loss of respect" for the administrator; RC defended the decision with an uncharacteristically agitated demeanor that I interpreted as "we had no choice," and teachers commented on the harshness of the official response. Ten days later, it was not a topic that emerged in my planned interviews.

Residence Life contends with adolescence and its manifestations of independence, experimentation, and sexuality. Residential Life enforces rules in a real and fuzzy world where multiple interpretations of an action are possible. Bright students are often skillful at having rationales for their actions. Teachers can speak hypothetically and critically about how to handle inappropriate social behavior. Counselors have no such luxury. Students act; RC must respond. Being Solomon is not easy. Residential Life tries to be responsive to individuals by the policy of RC autonomy, which leads to inconsistencies that haunt the place and generate frequent complaints.

DORM FLOORS AND ROOMMATE RELATIONSHIPS

Most action happens behind closed doors in a world that is hidden from adults. In the evenings the activity level reaches its height after study hours and after 12:30 when everyone is supposed to be sleeping. Often, throughout the day and night, as I walked down the hall I heard sounds inside, usually music or the smell of microwaved food seeping from under the door.

Considerable variation exists in the behavior on the floors and their wings. The floors set the context for much dorm behavior. The RC's personality has the strongest influence on behavior, followed by the way in which senior students distribute themselves. One senior girl remarked, "Last year's juniors are spread out as seniors on the floor so there is more interaction on the floor than is typical."

Floors have reputations. Certain rooms and floors seemed more attractive than others because of the people, the free food available, the RC, or the videogame or tape. A senior boy noted, "The fourth floor in both dorms is the more social floor. First floor stays to themselves; second floor is like theatre people, and third floor are people that like to study."

Students move freely from floor to floor in their own dorm, although not all students move off their floor often. A female senior commented, "I would not go to another floor unless I have homework and my partner on that floor." Movement within the dorm was more active on the boys' side than the girls'. Movement from the girl side to the boy side is limited by a key system. Sunday when people returned from the weekend at home was a time when some movement was more likely.

The plain, institutional-looking rooms are changed by students to fit their personalities. Most rooms look like any college room. Boys' rooms tend to be stuffed with more technology than the girls' rooms and often include videogame systems. A quick look would reveal a wide range of organization from neat to unbelievably messy on both sides.

Roommate preferences are honored when possible. Juniors have less choice because they are meeting strangers. Seniors may select both a roommate and a residence counselor. Relationships between roommates may be close friends, casual friends, or merely acquaintances. Among my eight prime participants, the variety was evident. One had all meals with the roommate and they spent free time together. Two other participants (a junior and a senior) told me they knew of their roommate prior to GI and this extended their relationship. Others told me they were sociable but not buddies. In two cases the roommate pair was minority-majority arrangement. One male volunteered that the key to "getting along [with your roommate] was not to be friends." Some roommates have differences that must be ignored or that demand negotiation. Two boys had an imaginary line in their room and the difference between sides of the room was obvious in terms of neatness and decor. Their tense relationship was known on both sides of the dorm.

THE RHYTHM OF DORM LIFE

The rhythms of residential life are either the routine behavior associated with living in a dorm or are attempts to physically and psychologically escape it. These interlaced and opposing rhythms of living and escaping can be seen in several patterns.

Leaving the Dorm Complex

Leaving the dorm happens all day, but here I am concerned about activity not connected with classes. The number of students that leave depends on the day of the week. Ordinarily about 30% to 45% leave the building each day after school for nonacademic activity. Leaving is a behavior with important significance; to some students it symbolizes freedom. It means, "I can get away from the rules and watchful eyes of the institution. I do not have a car, but I can get away."

When students leave, there is not much to do in the community and the rules for returning curtail much activity. Students mainly walk around, sometimes with a destination in mind. The walking ranges over a large area, including the university campus and the neighboring community. Most walking is toward the Village, a collection of stores typical for many college towns adjacent to the university, where there are places to eat and drink coffee and stores to buy books, CDs, food, cosmetics, and rent videos. A moderately popular destination in warm weather is a park beside a river, although it is "off limits." One advantage of the river is that it takes 20–30 minutes to walk to it. Students can also take buses to various places, but that rarely happens. On weekends some boys go walking to see where and how far they can go in the time allotted. One girl walked to a distant supermarket with her pack weekly. A small steady group of students leave to smoke.

A common reason to leave is to do something athletic. A small group regularly goes to the university gym to lift weights, work out, run, or participate on a sports team. Dating and sex are reasons to leave. One leaves the building to find a place to be alone. The open spaces on the campus as well as empty classrooms are waiting. The Quad is well used; the college buildings less so.

A special kind of sanctioned leaving is the "runs," which are organized, usually for food, mall shopping, or to see a movie at a theater. The RCs are collaborators because they drive the students to various locations and pick them up at a later time.

"HANGING OUT" IN FREE TIME

"Hanging out" often occurs when students leave the building. Hanging out at the broadest level is being with a friend, usually a group, with the purpose of getting away from typical or normal activity. "Normal" at the institute means doing academics, so hanging out means doing something nonacademic and avoiding homework. It does not have to mean literally leaving the building.

> I guess in essence hanging out is . . . kind of a way of getting away from things. The ways of hanging out have a connection, but there's different ways of doing it . . . getting away from the usual ways of doing things and doing what you like. And here the usual way of doing things is largely academic.

Activities may appear to be "hanging out," but they are not thought of as that by students. Romance could be part of hanging out, but actively dating couples infrequently use the term. Sports activities could also be considered hanging out, but, as one said, "It [gym] is necessary so it is not hanging out." Both of these fit closer to the meaning of leaving the building.

Some students see hanging out as connected to being in a place with others. For example, one hangs out with the RCs in their rooms or teachers in their offices or in the lounge. Most hanging out happens with peers anywhere.

> When I hang out with my friends, just practical jokes, making fun, having fun all the time. With my best friend, it's kind of the same thing, but on a deeper level, 'cause then it's just me and him going at it with different people. And hanging out with my girlfriend is just like going to the movies, going out to eat, and just talking on the phone.

A female junior states that hanging out occurs in the lounge while waiting for something to happen. "I think hanging out is to do something to not do homework, just anything with a group of people, avoiding doing homework." Some students do not describe themselves as hanging out much. They are too busy or do not define their actions as hanging out, but they know what it means.

Hanging out and leaving the building are connected in one significant way—they do not really achieve their purpose. Leaving the building and hanging out can help one get away from GI, but apparently only temporarily.

It's a lot of work here, I can't say it's just work, you know, it's like . . . there's no release from the GI life. No matter what you do, you're always thinking can I get wellness credit, you know, or maybe should I be doing homework instead of this, or, you know, since I have free time maybe I should call my parents, you know.

"STAYING UP LATE" IN THE DORM

Students have full days. They awaken, jump into their clothes, rush to classes, and are involved in various activities. When do they go to bed?

Adults and students have a different meaning for the phrase, "staying up late." The faculty and the RC have different definitions, too. The faculty and administration believe that after midnight constitutes staying up late. The RC thought staying up late for students was after 1:30. Students, on the other hand, had a different idea. A precise time for staying up late is not possible, "but two o'clock is not staying up late," said a male senior. "Staying up late is like four o'clock," opined a female junior who confirmed that 2:00 would "not be staying up late." While this general definition fits the school culture, some individuals consider time after midnight to be staying up late. Boys are more likely to be staying up than girls. Both boys and girls tell stories about being up late. Some of this difference is attributable to the custom in the boys' dorm of "screwing around" until 12:30. The fourth floor is the source of most stories in both dorms. One RC remarked in a Residence Life meeting that he would "bet $10 that none of my guys start homework until twelve-thirty." On the floor in which I lived, most were asleep by 2:00. Not being able to walk off my floor to confirm activity level in the dorm, I counted lights on in rooms from my window at intervals through the night.

Countless stories of staying up late are in the lore of the Greenhouse Institute. It is the common topic at meals. These stories merge with claims of staying up all night. Listening and questioning repeatedly point to the conclusion that the stories exceed the actual practice. During the semester, Sunday and Tuesday night are times when staying up late is more likely, but it is not the regular practice for most students. The range over a year is from zero to 25 times. In the same vein, I was unable to get a clear definition of what constituted an all-nighter. At GI, it seemed to involve going to sleep near dawn. Part of the staying up late may be linked to resistance to the rules of the institution.

EXPERIMENTING WITH NEW BEHAVIORS

At GI, meeting people who are different from one's usual experience is inevitable. One cannot avoid encountering behavior, values, and ideas that are new. Students try out all sorts of behavior, including new haircuts, styles of dressing, ways of talking, games, and eating. Changes in hair color or style are the most common for both sexes. The experimenting that is of most concern to GI adults involves experimenting with smoking, drugs, alcohol, and sex. Among these four behaviors, I have placed them in their order of frequency at GI from most to least.

No Smoking

One rule had a pervasive and perverse effect on the climate of the school: the no-smoking rule. Many forces are put into play by the rule. The GI official position on tobacco is that it is a legal issue. The use, sale, and distribution of tobacco to people under age 18 are illegal, with punishment and fines in the state in which GI is located. The official policy at GI is, "Break the rule; you are out of school." Nevertheless, students tested the rule.

No smoking pushes students out of the school to hidden places. Students who are 18 can legally smoke away from campus. Some arrive as smokers and it was permitted by their families. However, GI does not want students to smoke for any reason. Yet on the other hand, GI does not want to punish students for making bad choices by automatically dismissing them from school with no reprieve—the punishment would be too harsh for the crime. Therefore RCs tend to look the other way, much as the police do with some kinds of victimless crime.

In the midst of the adult rules are adolescents who judge smoking as a symbolic act of independence with minimal immediate health consequences and no real safety issues. In repeated interviews students indicated that smoking was done by many of them. Many tried it out, but relatively few were serious smokers. Residence Life developed a three-tiered policy so that when students were "written up," they could choose to go through an educational process before dismissal.

The ways to get around the smoking ban were common knowledge, planned, and funny. Places existed around campus where students would walk to smoke, such as the parking garage in inclement weather or the park or even the roof of the dorm. Rooms had fans, ostensibly to remove heat from poorly air-conditioned or overheated rooms that were used to extract smoke. One student was caught when he mistakenly had the fan turned into the room and blew smoke under his door out into the dorm hall.

FOOD, FORAGING, AND NOT HOME COOKING

Adolescents eat at any time. Besides the official meal schedule that fits into the university dining plan, students spend much of their free time foraging or preparing food in their rooms. When not sleeping, studying, or hanging out, students are usually eating. In fact, eating is often a combined or integrated part of hanging out or studying. Junk food is king.

The official time to eat as set by the dining hall schedule is: breakfast 6:30–9:30; lunch 10:30–1:30; dinner 4:30–6:30. On weekends, the dining hall is open for 4 hours each day with no breakfast on Saturday. Those hours allow for personal preferences, as well as for schedules filled with classes. Students may arrange to pick up a bag lunch if they cannot make it to the dining hall.

The meals are nutritious and food is plentiful. According to college students, this dining hall (which they share) is "the best kept secret on campus." Returning for seconds is part of the game. GI students compare what they are eating and some go back to try what their friends had. As would be expected, the food typically receives unflattering reviews. This is "not home cooking." For omnivores, as some call each other, there is variety. For vegetarians, and even more so for vegans, finding something to eat is sometimes difficult. "I'm a vegetarian so it's a little bit more challenging to find things to eat at Dining Service," said one senior as she bemoaned the fate of her vegan friends at lunch one Saturday. Some students actively avoid eating in the dining hall—they either eat in their rooms or go out to eat. The latter is only an option for well-to-do students. Betsy, a junior, claimed that after September she "never ate dinner" at GI. She simply walked to nearby restaurants and returned in time for study hours.

Meals are a social occasion. But the pressure of homework, full schedules of classes, and the attraction of other activities means socializing happens fast while eating. Students eat fast and leave. Twenty minutes is the average time spent eating. Dinner lasts longer than other meals because most people do not have to be someplace else shortly.

People sit where they want. There is a flow of people in and out of groups. Conversations are about topics that pertain to life at the school. Breakfast conversations are about staying up late, studying or some incident, or a class later in the day. Lunch conversations are similar, although filled with more zany humor in the form of wordplay or talk about a topic on the Internet. At dinner when there is more time, conversation about the quality of the food, unfair rules and punishment, whether the food that night is or is not bad, classes or a class topic, and pranks are discussed, indicating that students share information to which adults are not privy. The conversation is quick, cerebral, and tolerant of outlandish statements about political or social events, replete with sexual references, and it roams around multiple topics. During weekends the talk is slower, more leisurely. On Monday one hears stories being shared about weekend activities that involve sleeping, studying or not studying, partying, and home life.

In most dorm rooms there is a microwave and a refrigerator stocked with food and drink. At the start of study sessions time, I have seen students carrying water to rooms to make soup or a hot drink, even though dinner had officially ended. Students returning from a weekend home commonly enter GI carrying bags filled with food through the lounge. "Stocking up?" "Yeah, I'm ready for the week," was the smug reply. Students develop reputations for having certain foods, and know whom to approach. Some students go home every weekend and are great sources of supplemental nourishment for their friends.

Foraging activities are evident in many ways. Students walk to the Village to buy food in fast-food venues like Subway, Burger King, or supermarkets. "Runs" are a frequent foraging activity. As mentioned before, the term refers to going somewhere with an RC in a vehicle. Runs vary in length. The longest I experienced was a run to a town 35 minutes away for ice cream and whatever else the student wanted to eat. A shorter run would be nightly "Bell runs" to Taco Bell. The residence counselors stock junk food. Students, in and outside a specific RC's group, drop in for a handout and conversation throughout the afternoon and evening, much like the grazing that occurs in the evenings in clubs. RCs also have a budget from GI that can be used for various activities with the students. Usually that means getting snack food or cake to celebrate a birthday or some event. I recall visiting a female RC room when on "rounds" with a male RC between 8:00 and 10:00 and she was having a "cocktail party" with her girls, which meant canapes, fruity-looking drinks in tall glasses, and party hats.

A TYPICAL BUSY EVENING

The pace of activity as well as the overlap between school and dorm is evident in residential life. In the evenings the rhythms of both intertwine to create another time filled with activity. To illustrate the situation, I include an edited selection from my field notes to show that the students are active and the pace of GI life persists throughout the day.

At 8:00 p.m., I head for the lounge downstairs like other students. Thirty sign out for the gym (swimming, weight lifting, soccer, volley-ball). Three couples leave. In the lounges, a few are playing pool, "messing" with the piano, or just talking. Fifteen more students join the sign-out parade. Two girls enter carrying cokes and other food from shopping and sign-in, followed by about 30 more who are signing in from the "AP Chem. Test" that was held that evening.

Tonight is Wednesday, Interviz night, a special RA-initiated program of visitation where students can cross the gender divide in the dorm. A female RA monitors the door and six girls register to go upstairs. Later, in my wandering I see three of the girls in a male RC's room where a mixed group is watching a video and talking.

Off to the left, outside the faculty offices, some students are sitting on the floors by the open doors waiting to talk to teachers.

Going upstairs too, I stop in my RC's room as several guys play darts and watch the Dallas-Philadelphia football game. Everyone is eating Fritos. Bill, a junior, alternates playing computer solitaire, darts and watching the game. Boys drop in from all over the dorm to check the score and eat. A few sit, eat chips for a minute and move on. Franklyn, an RC, looks in, makes a wisecrack as he goes down the hall to a club meeting he sponsors in the Conference Room.

At 9:00 Sam and I sign out for the Village. Looking in the stores and shops, no GI students are seen. Buying coffee, we return and sign in. I learn some fourth floor boys are having a contest later, after 12:30 to see who can drink the most coffee.

Tonight between 10:30–12:30 during hall hours, wing (not floor) meetings have been called. My RC explains the forthcoming extended weekend. Afterwards, I wander around visiting rooms with open doors, playing videogames, eating, and talking. My floor mates talk about girls, courses, the coffee drinking contest, etc. Some doors are closed. A few boys start to get ready for bed by walking down the hall to wash up before the 12:30 curfew. I return to my room. It gets quiet. I can hear doors opening and closing softly. A few remain in

the floor study lounge, which is permitted. Students have told me,
"You live on a quiet floor."

Sharing this small section of field notes was meant to illustrate typical activity level. A student can be busy or move at any pace he or she wants. This night was far from the busiest.

THE WORLD SLOWS DOWN ON WEEKENDS

Weekends begin when a student's classes end on Friday. Students return to the dorm to prepare to go home or to do heavy relaxing. Weekends are a slower simpler time. The hustle of the schedule filled with classes, meetings, and clubs is removed. Weekends are a time for refueling, catching up, and getting ready for the next week. Weekends are also a time for getting into trouble and finding out more about oneself. Weekends are a source of some of GI's most talked-about stories.

The basic elements of GI life are still happening, but are in suspended animation. A male junior stated

> But up until like twelve-thirty [p.m.] it's kind of like fend for yourself.
> You go outside and you do the same things that you do on week-
> nights, basically. I mean that's what we do, we go try and find a
> restaurant and basically the only difference is that you don't have the
> pressure of knowing that you have homework to do.

Weekends come in two varieties: normal and extended. I'll talk first about "extendeds." During these times, the school shuts down and students and residential counselors go home. Extended weekends provide opportunities for students to return home during months when a vacation is not scheduled. It is part of the Greenhouse Institute's recognition of the nonacademic needs of students.

Students told me that extendeds occurred so they could get relief from the school and to make their parents happy. Many students take the opportunity to visit their home school and friends. Much laundry gets transported home. Students welcome home cooking, their old bed, and old friends.

Extendeds also produce discomfort. Some students return to environments (home, school, or community) where they were not particularly happy. They have to deal with issues such as family strife, dangerous neighborhoods, few friends, and so forth. As time goes by, seniors report more distance with their former peers, which produces mixed feelings. Interestingly, juniors begin to realize that the Greenhouse Institute is becoming their home, as noted earlier.

When the "normal" weekends begin, the feeling is immediately more relaxed. Some rules are relaxed. For example, three girls are playing foosball, something that is normally prohibited at 3:00 in the afternoon, yet a passing RC says nothing.

The student body is split at this time between those who stay and those who go home. Students go home for a variety of reasons, such as missing a boyfriend, church, escape from GI rules, and the desire to engage in risky behaviors. A few go because they are sent home and excluded from weekend activity as a punishment for misbehavior. A story that floats around is that some parents want their children to come home to study. An individual's pattern of staying or leaving on a weekend changes over the 2 years at GI and within a semester. A senior told me he could not sleep his junior year and now he sleeps 12 hours. The same person stayed most weekends as a junior and since Thanksgiving has been going home weekly. Frederick has gone home for three quarters of the weekends this semester: "I like to hang with my friends and here people mainly sleep and I like to be doing something."

Students stay because they like GI better and prefer not to be home under family rules and strife. Some, like Rosa, always stay because of distance from home and lack of funds to take transportation home. However, Rosa has another reason. Waiting at the desk, the RC on duty asks, "Do you want Billy's (her boyfriend) card, too?" Rosa nods and says yes. Thus, the opportunity for the couple to be together for the longest time possible at the Greenhouse Institute begins.

Students characterize staying at GI for the weekend as, "Boring!" and "It sucks!" The general meaning is, "There is nothing [exciting] to do!" Interestingly, students characterize weekends at home before coming to GI the same way. The restriction of movement—meaning no car and an enforced curfew—bothers them.

Friday starts the weekend in the dorm.

> We don't have study sessions Friday so we can like leave at six-thirty and be out until eleven-thirty, which is cool. But still, it's like we basically have nothing to do. So we bum around just normally like we would on like a school day. So, you know, it's just leaving the building for really just no purpose.

In the lounges on Friday there is ceaseless movement. Friends greet each other, moving over to make room on the couch quietly and leave again. Meanwhile, a movie is showing in the corner of the lounge. In the nearby computer room students are checking e-mail, searching the Web, and playing videogames. Two boys carry athletic gym equipment on their way to the gym. Some students go to bed early, but most stay up until the small hours of the morning.

The basic weekend pattern is sleep, eat, "hang out," go on "runs" for food or movies, walk around, participate in hall programs, and stay in one's room. Some students spend the whole weekend catching up on the academic work. Peter tells me, "Jim [his roommate] goes home so I sleep late, catch up on my homework, play video games and take it easy." Almost everyone sleeps late. Many sleep into the afternoon of both days, following talking until 4:00 a.m. or later on Friday and Saturday night. Breakfast has few students on Saturday and a few more on Sunday who eat before going to church or to study. Lunch has more attendance, and dinner even more. One Saturday when the Scholastic Aptitude Test (SAT) was given, large numbers were up and out. The slower weekend pace begins to speed up on Sunday with the prospect of classes ahead.

Saturday and Sunday start quietly and remain that way until the early afternoon. Around 1:30 or so, the student residence assistants and/or the RC have dorm programs for those who want to participate. They include contests modeled after Family Feud, a reading of *Winnie the Pooh*, a crafts activity like drawing, and so forth. Attendance is sparse.

WEEKENDS ARE OPPORTUNITIES FOR GETTING INTO TROUBLE

RCs work to keep track of where everyone is, but that is an impossible task. Throughout the day, students sign in and out. RCs are asked to go on various runs. These are more than the usual food-foraging activity. They may ferry students to the mall for shopping, to a movie theater, or take them on an excursion to a park. Some runs are preannounced for people to sign up and others are more spontaneous. Being able to persuade an RC into a run is a skill. Some RCs are reputed to be more amenable than others. By 11:30 all are back in the dorm, although most have been there for hours. A senior girl reported,

> We come up [stairs] at eleven-thirty depending on whatever. The
> people that are in relations basically stay down until twelve-thirty
> and like I'll stay down there if something's happening, or like if I'm
> in a conversation with someone, but usually I don't have any reason
> to be down there after eleven-thirty on weekends.

The later curfew makes it possible to stay out longer, but students do not really have that many options on Friday or Saturday. A few students try to get included in the university social party scene, although that is against the rules. Those efforts rarely work as anticipated, some seniors indicated, "because even if you go to a frat party, like you gotta be back at eleven-thirty . . . I don't think frat parties really get going at eleven-thirty [some laughter]." Students who want to use alcohol or drugs find them at GI just like they do in their home schools. Experimentation does occur. Stories abound but they involve only a small percentage of the students. Despite all the work to interrupt it, GI is an opportune place to try out some risky behavior, although I heard of no peer pressure to do so. Instead, I learned of instances where students tried "only once."

Around 12:30 female students can cross the gender divide of the dorm to go to a male RC's room, usually to watch videos. These can go on until 2:30 in some cases. Students are escorted back to their dorm by an RC. During this time those who are not watching a movie are talking, playing videogames, et cetera, in rooms in groups of various sizes. Some students in each dorm are visiting floors that are not where their room is located. They go to hang out and talk. It is up to the RCs whether they can remain later than 2:30. Many stories are told of sleeping on someone's floor because the doors to the floors are locked.

AN ORDINARY, SPECIAL WEEKEND EXPERIENCE

The ordinary relaxed pace of the weekend sets up conditions for interactions that illustrate intense special experiences that happen at GI. They also happen during the week, but are less likely to then because of the fast pace of each weekday. The students who leave to go home for the weekend miss these moments.

Those "cool" moments occur at times when students are hanging out talking and something happens that makes GI much different than the regular school, as noted by one junior male:

> *Student:* There are times when it's like you are just sitting there and like start talking about an issue and, you know, just maybe discuss some philosophy or something. I mean that's usually cool, the fact that education is not always going on in the classroom, 'cause it goes on other places too, you know?
> *Larry:* Mm-hmm, is this one of the ways you might say that the Academy is different?
> *Student:* Yeah. There are more chances for it to happen. Like when you're . . . locked on to your floor at twelve-thirty on the weekends, then, like, you know that nobody's going to be in the rooms, so you're wandering around talking to people. And like,

you get these really close bonds formed, and then like, you
know you can have like these really intense discussions, like
intellectual, you know. And so . . . you could not have that back
home. . . .

Larry: And these things happen more on weekends than they do
during the week.

Student: Yeah, I would say so. 'Cause during the week, people are
most likely concerned with homework.

IS RESIDENTIAL LIFE A REFUGE?

If your impression of residential life is that it is a refuge from the demands
of the Greenhouse Institute, then this section should change your view. The
demand on student time is not solely academic. Residential Life exerts stress
of its own through "mandatory time," a students' term to describe the Wellness
program and the service program, which comprise nonacademic graduation
requirements. The latter is also academic in orientation, but I include it here
as a component of residential life because students spoke of them together.
Within any week many GI-sanctioned activities are available. Among that
large number, some are mandatory and others are voluntary. Because these
activities take time and time is a limited commodity, these requirements are
not a minor concern of students. Opinions about the requirements vary among
the students. Some find the service programs and Wellness program to be
beneficial, while others resent, and are often angry, about the time spent in
those activities.

    "Mandatory Time" activities are intended to build commitment to the
GI community values. Service activities are designed to build an investment
in the institute community and/or the hometown community. The idea is
that students are members of the GI community and are still members of
their home communities, so they should make a contribution to each. Wellness
activities are intended to promote a well-adjusted, healthy lifestyle.

    The service programs are mandatory volunteering opportunities. The
Community service program is done on holidays, on weekends, and in the
summer, away from GI. The Greenhouse Institute service program involves
students participating in the running of GI by engaging in activities such as
assisting teachers, the admissions office, workers at the computer lab, and
so forth. Students make many more positive comments about Greenhouse
Institute service than Community service, although some students report that
Community service opened their eyes to new career possibilities.

    One kind of service that earns institutional credit is connected to being
a Residence Assistant (RA). RAs have an important role in the institution

because they function as liaisons to their peers and as role models. RAs regularly meet on Monday evenings under the guidance of a male and female RC. The group discusses issues, builds community, offers some Wellness programs and does service projects of their own. One such project at Christmastime involved helping impoverished children in the city located near the Greenhouse Institute. An interesting feature of the RA group is that some went home most weekends, so they do not participate in aspects of GI community life.

The Wellness program is the most complex of the mandatory time requirements. "Wellness" has been part of GI since its founding. The Wellness program originates from a specialty in counseling known as College Student Personnel Counseling, a university program participated in by many of the residential counselors. Similar counselor preparation programs are found on many campuses. The premise is to promote the well-being of people by having them engage in a variety of activities.

At GI the program translates into students being required to earn "wellness credits" in order to graduate. The Wellness program involves its own curricular model. I encountered the Wellness bulletin board my first day on campus. Seniors were reminded that they had "9 weeks to complete their junior wellness credits."

Graduation hinged on completion of these credits. These categories, and the number of credits one needed to earn, are listed with a brief definition of the category:

5 — cultural (experiencing different cultures),
5 — diversity (experiencing different values),
5 — emotional (exploring feelings and self),
5 — social (exploring your social self),
2 — physical (using your body),
2 — vocational (exploring careers),
6 — electives.

The definitions between categories were an issue the entire time I was at the school.

Students must participate in wellness experiences, which are small programs offered by residence counselors or residence assistants, as well as special programs offered by teachers, speaking guests, and so forth. For example, participating in a discussion sponsored by the Black Student Union about the movie *Higher Learning* would earn a diversity credit. Listening to a speaker from the local medical college would earn vocational credit. Going to the art museum would earn cultural credit. Residence Assistants are expected to offer three programs each semester: wing program, floor program, and whole GI program. A form must be completed for credits to be awarded. Many students resent the procedures and the demand on their time. The well-intentioned program produces paradoxical effects in GI life. Much more about this program appears in the next chapter.

CONCLUSION

Residential life is half of life at the Greenhouse Institute, which psychologically takes up more than 50% of the time. In conjunction with academic life, RL creates the student experience. GI becomes home for students, though this new home is not like a normal home. Routines and comfort are upset. Diversity of race, religion, ideas, and values is everywhere. Rules that are institutional rather than personal govern behavior. A group of strangers monitors behavior, ostensibly to protect students and help them make wise choices. Students accept the statements, even see benefit in them, but doubt the approach. Residence counselors have the task of enforcing rules using discretion based upon more complete knowledge of their students. Students complain about inconsistency, rigidity, and lack of individuality. Dorm life has rhythms—eating, sleeping, socializing, and experimenting. Weekends bring a break in the fast pace. They are a time for relaxing, catching up, and sleeping. Weekends are also a time for experimenting with new behaviors and getting into trouble and learning more about oneself. Residence counselors have exhausting weekends monitoring the activity. Residential Life accommodates most student needs. At the same time RL, with its rules and requirement, adds subtle pressures to the already intense life of students at the Greenhouse Institute.

CHAPTER SIX

Looking Deeper into the Fast Lane

Social settings like the Greenhouse Institute are pregnant with multiple meanings. In previous chapters I described the students' experience, but I left out parts of the story until now, when understanding is broad enough to sustain a more complex interpretation. I am filling in spaces that deserve more attention in order to convey the subtle meanings of having a residential school where potential meets opportunity. More specifically, I examine the implicit contradictions in the setting. I expand on the Wellness program, rules and rule bending, educational malnourishment, student resistance to GI, and the meaning and the value of curriculum content.

LIVING AND LEARNING IN THE FAST LANE

The Greenhouse Institute experience occurs in an environment that brings academically talented adolescent peers together to learn in a rigorous academic program taught by teachers who love their content, all while living in a residential setting. Challenging classes with the relentless demand of homework combined with the mandatory nonacademic credits for graduation quickly fill up students' time. The pace of life is inescapable and time is finite. Choosing to be at GI means students bring an orientation to self that heightens the experience for all in an already intense environment. The intersection of student and school yields an exciting experience where students are compelled to grow. Living in the fast lane means rushing forward, confronting challenging ideas, and trying new behaviors toward some elusive state of becoming that extends to future schooling. The GI pull is intrusive. Whether hanging out, sleeping, or simply daydreaming, thoughts of having to complete an assignment or mandatory requirements are on the minds of students. Students are carried forward by the academic and nonacademic demands toward graduation—enter one year, leave the next, keep your foot on the accelerator.

WELLNESS AND GRADUATION REQUIREMENTS

In this complex institution I encountered paradoxical policies that fostered behaviors that seemed to contradict the mission of the Greenhouse Institute. These policies are the intrusion of values from mainstream society into this special environment that distort the development of academic talent. Understanding one such policy, Graduation and Wellness Requirements, and the students' interpretation of it is necessary in order to appreciate life at GI.

The Greenhouse Institute asks students to complete graduation requirements that go beyond those needed for a state-approved graduation. The Wellness and the Service programs are the source of much contention and distortion in the institution. "Wellness," as it is called by students, illustrates the philosophical contradictions that coexist in the Greenhouse Institute. In Wellness students have the opportunity to participate in hundreds of small special activities offered throughout the year that earn credits toward graduation. Activities are advertised as a way to earn credit. The reporting procedures and the time it takes create mixed feelings about the entire GI program among students and some residence counselors and teachers, as well. A junior states the student viewpoint:

> [Wellness is] just the institute's way of piling all this homework on you and they want you to stay well-rounded, they don't want you to be just academic. But they don't give you enough time to do that. . . . You have to have so many wellness credits, but you have so much homework to do and you can't do it. You can't get it all in . . . The whole thing is, you have these wellness slips that you have to fill out for everything. You've got your name, the date, and you can give some stupid reason for doing it. This one [in my hand] was for Bible study and that comes under emotional/spiritual wellness. I can't turn that in because you have only three days to turn it in. It is really annoying because you forget about it. Like I have no physical [wellness credits] right now, just because I don't fill it out. It's just . . . a pain. I go out every night. Whenever I go out, I don't feel like saying, hey, I need to fill out a wellness slip for that two hours that we walked around tonight. You're not thinking about that.

Many seniors echo those less than positive comments. To them, wellness means more work in an already busy schedule, a complicated reporting system, attention to areas of life for which they have little interest and not getting credit for activities that they consider wellness.

A much smaller number of students value Wellness as a means to relieve themselves of the self-generated pressure of academics. A senior noted,

> Sometimes it gets to the point where students get tunnel vision and the only thing is academics, your classes, and homework. A student may sort of need that excuse to go do something else. It's like wellness is a graduation requirement. So . . . I'm not really slacking off. And it kind of gives an excuse, I don't know if that's the right word, but to get rid of some stress, just do something different and get out of the room.

Residential Life staff welcomes statements like this senior's. Widespread concern exists among RCs that GI students are too concentrated on academics. The comment fits their rationale for the program. Wellness is intended for students to become more aware of options and to have a more balanced lifestyle, which adds up to a healthier life. Not all RCs share this view completely. The doubters about the program worry that the Wellness Program forces students to fit into a mold that may be unnatural for some of them.

The program, as stated by students, sets up barriers to attaining wellness, especially with the reporting process. RCs recognize that students spontaneously engage in activities that resemble official wellness activities for which they do not get credit. For example, intellectual discussions that can spring up at any time do not count unless they are planned. "It is one of the things I kind of looked forward to [before coming to GI] and it happened!" a junior noted. But it is not recognized. Another common example of a spontaneous wellness activity would be students who read books unconnected to schoolwork. These activities are more organic and valid to students than many wellness experiences. As one senior observed, "Students should get credit for things that actually they did to make themselves well. Running after the accumulation of points often conflicts with attaining wellness." By the last 2 weeks of the school year in May, 13 students had not earned any credits, as indicated on a public bulletin board. The pressure was on those students who were seniors since completing the Wellness program is part of the GI graduation requirement.

Could the positively intentioned Wellness program influence adults and students to act contrary to its purpose? Consider these possibilities. Students find many of the categories uninteresting or meaningless and question why they cannot get credit for wellness they do for themselves. Wellness activities have low priority in comparison to homework. For this reason students procrastinate. As deadlines approach, they scramble for credits as the residence counselors struggle to invent programs to fill in the categories. Meanwhile, among the adults, the same questions are raised. Some question the meaning of the categories, the appropriateness of the experiences, and the administrative procedures, too. Toward the end of the school year adults award credits very liberally in order to help students accumulate wellness credits, because the penalty of nongraduation seems too severe. Juniors see seniors' behavior, and adults' reactions question further the idea that wellness has much value. Why should I do them, when I can squeeze them in at the end of the year? Students know that adults will help them evade the requirement. Adults who do not function as RCs are not opposed to the program, but the strongest statement of support I could find was that the Wellness program does no harm and it helps some kids so we should keep it. I return to Wellness as a topic in Chapter 8 to illustrate the deeper meaning of this practice.

RULE BENDING: SOFTENING THE LIVED WORLD

Living at the Greenhouse Institute is an intense experience. The pace and rigor of the courses keep students on edge. In addition, GI is almost a total institution (Goffman, 1961), which means all aspects of living are controlled by the authorities. I say almost because students do have some choices, one of which is withdrawal.

Amidst this pressure, the GI experience is softened by unofficial interpersonal interactions. Without them, GI might become an unforgiving place. The need to manage a large group often comes in conflict with individual needs. Officially, there are procedures and policies that build in attention to the individual, such as the Retention and Dismissal Committee, RC discretion, a clinical psychologist on staff, and community meetings that are the institutional attempts to be sensitive.

The unofficial efforts of adults to soften the situation are most interesting because they put a human face on what is sometimes viewed by students as an impersonal environment. Most of these actions seem to fit under rule bending, which means rules or policies are circumvented, ignored, or broken. In some instances it is a personal policy stated by a person in authority. In other instances it is an official policy.

A great deal of rule bending by teachers is related to time and their awareness of the many time-consuming academic demands that students face. All schedules are not created equal. Teachers also recognize that students place themselves in situations by the way they commit to a task. Teachers have rules for their classes as to when homework and major assignments are due, but considerable flexibility is introduced into the academic system by modifying or suspending the rules. Often, the time homework is to be handed in is changed from class time to the end of the day or to office hours. Students have strategies for asking for extensions on homework, and all reported that teachers understand the situation. So stated deadlines are usually not the real deadline.

Assignments are also modified to meet individual needs. A teacher might drop an assignment for one child and substitute another. Or a teacher might completely alter course requirements for a student in an effort to "differentiate instruction." Some teachers do not grade homework. An instance of official policy being stretched is taking attendance and not reporting it to the central office. Many teachers do this sporadically. Classes are set to begin at set times. Arrival has more flexibility than is apparent from the syllabus. This is especially true in the 8:00 a.m. classes.

The residence counselors bend rules, too. I have already spoken of altering the school study session to meet students' needs and of their help in accumulating wellness and service credits. The physical arrangements make this obvious. Another way in which RCs are responsive and bend a policy is that they agree to sponsor clubs around students' interests even though the counselor has no personal interest in the topic.

At GI there are other adults who are neither counselors nor teachers who work with the students and introduce a softening element. On one day I observed the nurse violating her own rule and granting a student, who seemed stressed out, a medical excuse. In another instance, the guidance counselor created a support group for students with learning disabilities to help them deal with the demands of scheduling and homework.

The final group that works to lighten the pressure is, of course, the students. A lot of hanging out helps in this regard. Two examples that were becoming part of GI practice originated from student requests to soften the rules. The first is working to start inter-visitation, or "Interviz," a program of supervised visiting across the gender divide in the dorm one night per week. A second example is senior privilege, a program that grants seniors who are successful students a waiver of the sign-in/sign-out rule before study sessions.

EDUCATIONAL MALNOURISHMENT

Students entering the Greenhouse Institute do not have equal prior educational experience. Students who arrive with insufficient relevant educational experiences that inhibit their learning opportunities at the school are educationally malnourished. These holes in their experience are a by-product of the nature of their home school and community as well as the economic circumstance of the family. The lack of knowledge and skills is not due to ability, but rather circumstance. Students who fit this label most often come from urban and rural areas. Given the pace and depth of coursework, such students are at a disadvantage. Educational malnourishment is most evident in math and science classes, less so in humanities and language.

Placement in mathematics classes is determined by a test. Because the math courses are tightly sequenced and the more advanced classes are challenging, admittance is denied if one enters the school with insufficient math background. In this way educational malnourishment creates a loose form of tracking. Once a student starts in a less advanced class, he or she will be less likely to get to the most advanced class in the 2-year time frame of GI life. Exceptions to this situation are possible with extra work by a student and a teacher. Two examples of this are shown in my field notes, although it is possible that more was happening.

In humanities classes, evidence of educational malnourishment is seen in responses to reading, in the facility to incorporate broad experiences to fit the topic, and in limited vocabulary in classes. However, in humanities classes, educational malnourishment is less obvious to others because of the looser sequencing of classes. Teachers note this disparity and students, too, are aware that others have more or less knowledge.

The meaning of educational malnourishment to students is intriguing because all the students were selected through a deliberative process. Naturally, variations in ability are present, but all are competent, high-ability students. "Everyone here is smart," commented a senior. I wondered how students, both the educationally malnourished and those who are not, make sense of this situation. Almost all GI students did not have to work hard in their home schools, and meeting the demands of GI shows them they must work or they will not be able to stay.

Educationally malnourished students are hit with a double whammy. The malnourished students see their peers, even roommates, taking courses that are reputed to be challenging. Educationally malnourished students must wonder, "If peers are taking those courses, then what kind of courses am I in? What does that mean about me?" The irony is that the answer cannot be known. Judgment of one's ability is based on incomplete evidence. No students stated that they were not smart, yet students state that they are at the top in one class and in the middle or lower in another. Those who are educationally enriched looked at the situation as an example of natural variation; those who are educationally malnourished have trouble reconciling the situation.

My interpretation is that the malnourished students underestimate the strength of their own abilities and doubt themselves. I recall an undernourished student who took extra courses, struggled mightily to get into the more advanced sections, and drove himself to be successful. In the last weeks of his senior year, he appeared to undergo a transformation in demeanor upon learning he had been admitted to his first-choice college.

NEGATIVE REACTIONS, PRANKS, AND RESISTANCE

Initially, juniors find GI to be the place where they want to be. A few leave in the first weeks because GI separates them from friends and family in a way that they do not want or did not anticipate. Another group leaves because they cannot handle the demands of a rigorous academic schedule and the independence of dorm life throughout the year. A few leave, I was told by other students, because they resent the regimentation and policies of GI. While I respect my informants who shared this view, I was not able, given my methods and resources, to corroborate that view by speaking directly with those who left. I accept the authenticity of the statements, but I think of them as examples of students blustering against the institutional demands and their conflicting feelings about them.

I am certain that many students who graduate harbored periodic negative feelings about the Greenhouse Institute. Students told me that they were considering leaving because of something that had happened. None left. I suspect a kind of love-hate duality develops in some of the students' thinking about the school. After all, GI is life in the fast lane. It is an intense, high-energy environment that is attractive, exhausting, exhilarating, and frustrating as students confront their own limits and discover new strengths.

Negative reactions that I define as acts of resistance to the GI policy and procedure are part of the story. Because students choose to be at GI, acts of resistance are a particularly interesting window into the school. Far more students engage in resistance than the small number who might have left in anger or frustration.

The enforcement of rules is an obvious expression of adult authority. Students rub up against the rules, which generate common kinds of resistance in most students. I define resistance as conscious action to circumvent or disrupt policies and practices of the institution. Acts of resistance are more than not abiding by the rules—resistance involves intention. Resistance, in my terms, is more than the generalized reaction against adult authority that we assume is the role of adolescents in our society. The rare exceptions among students who do not resist are those who do their own thing, are very compliant, or can rationalize putting off their nonacademic passions. When certain lightning-rod issues emerged—for example, room searches— some students would react by proclaiming we agreed to live by certain rules when we came so "it is no big deal," while another group would rail against the "invasion" of autonomy and privacy. So particular policies and rules have symbolic significance to students, as does resistance. In fact, for a subgroup of boys an icon—a toilet—is passed down from class to class to symbolize resistance. Interestingly, not every student is aware of the icon and neither are most adults.

A Continuum of Resistance

Mixed into acts of resistance are pranks that might not be instances of resistance, depending on the person's intention. In the lore of the school some pranks stand out as examples to students of daring, such as entering utility tunnels under the campus from shafts in the dorm walls. I put pranks on a continuum with fun at one end and sending messages of resistance to authority at the other.

At the fun end is a prank that is intended to draw attention to the instigator. One example would be "penny locking," which is a way of putting pennies in a doorjam so the door cannot be opened. Another example is collecting packages of condiments from fast food restaurants or appearing in two places in the official GI photograph of the school taken on opening day. These acts are not wanted by the school, rarely have sanctions attached to them, and are more like a sign saying "I am here" rather than "Screw you."

In the middle of the continuum is an action that appears harmless and fun yet is an indirect statement to adult authority that says, "We can do our own thing, but we will go along with your rules." For example, in the last month of the year the school awakened to a sign on the top of the academic building written in huge letters: "GI rules." The significant part of the prank is that it was conceived and executed by senior students who were mostly residence assistants, a sign of recognition of responsibility by adults.

A prank that moves further toward the resistant end would be one that demonstrates that students cannot be dismissed as being powerless. Examples are missing doors and pieces of furniture or the indiscriminant use of the Internet for illicit activity like viewing pornographic sites or annoying foreign embassies. The war with the dining service is the most obvious. A rule was made that GI students could no longer carry their bookbags into the serving and eating areas of the dining hall. The administration's story was that it was an attempt to stop people from taking food and dinnerware. Students complained that they were being singled out from the college students who shared the dining room, but to no avail. Silverware began to disappear. An announcement was made to return the silverware, but it remained hidden in an empty desk in the dorm until the end of the year.

Resistance is actions that clearly violate rules. There is no mistaking that a rule or policy is being ignored. Acts of resistance are often not known to

most adults, and also not known until later by many students. If the perpe-
trators were known, they would be punished.

Common resistant acts are linked to rules associated with time limits on
student behavior. The most frequent act is to ignore the sign-in/sign-out rules.
These are rules that GI has created to be able to monitor where students are
during the day. The flaunting of the rule was aided by the haphazard way it
was enforced and the inconvenience of having to return to report. Countless stories of students unintentionally breaking the rule, getting caught, and
being unfairly punished are shared. When I first heard comments like "I
forgot," "I did not mean to . . . ," I accepted them at face value. However,
the pervasiveness of the phenomenon of being caught more than once led
me to infer an act of resistance.

A related sign of resistance to a time-related rule occurred in relation to
curfew rules that mandate that students must be in their dorm by a certain
time and stay in the dorm until the next morning. Not having the liberty to
come and go as they pleased was especially bothersome to students. When
GI installed TV monitors in entrances and hallways to prevent intruders as
well as students leaving unsupervised, the students interpreted them as an
act of control and an evidence of distrust. Again students complained and
many were dissatisfied with the administrative response. For some students
the response was to plan to "break out" of the dorm undetected at various
times. Most of those plans were wishful thinking, and were never carried
out. Some plans were successfully executed in that they were not detected.
Leaving through a window was one strategy. Some students climbed to the
roof; others left the building early in the morning; still others left at night.
One student told me about rappelling down the wall of the dorm, hearing
voices, and hiding for the rest of the night under a bush to avoid detection.
Another act done during the day involved a group of students leaving the
campus and going to another town for the day. In total, only a small number really do these extreme actions.

The most contested and controversial act of resistance to adult authority
and state law was the no-smoking rule, discussed earlier. All smoking was an
act of defiance. The extent to which students organized to avoid detection
makes smoking an example of an act of resistance. Several locations, sprinkled
around campus not far from the dorm, were where students went to smoke
during the day and evenings. Most students brought fans, some very large
and powerful, ostensibly to cool off dorm rooms. Many fans were turned
outward to exhaust smoke, an observation that implies intention. In one instance a coffee can overflowing with cigarette butts was found in one room.
The dangerous attraction of smoking might have been increased because the
school had a humane policy that gave students a second chance if they were
caught instead of the immediate dismissal implied in the state law.

The use of alcohol and drugs were other examples of defiant acts done on a small scale. Most of these instances were experimental. Students knew others did it, but the peer culture would not report it. Knowledge of drugs is a sign of sophistication in the larger teenage culture. The amount of substance abuse was reported by students to be comparable or less than in their local high schools.

Sanctioned Resistance

Sanctioned resistance is resistance of which adults approve. This form of resistance overlaps with rule softening. A club called Institute Students for Constructive Criticism (ISCC), a pseudonym, was formed the year before I arrived. The ISCC represents organized sanctioned resistance to the policies and rules of the place. Members conducted their own survey to gather student opinion about homework and residential policies. Active members met to discuss and present alternatives to GI policy and practice. Members wanted GI to be an ideal place for learning. The group appeared to be losing cachet as the founders neared graduation.

RESISTANCE TO ACADEMICS

Because students who value academics must make a special effort to attend the Greenhouse Institute, resistance to academics is an important phenomenon to understand. Up to now, the resistance I have described has been to residential life. In the section on doing homework, I reported that students adjusted to the workload, especially overload in various ways, but I did not speak of resistance at that time. My decision was purposeful because I believe that *adjustment* is the better term for characterizing almost all students' actions. However, the manner in which a minority of students approached the homework and the way in which they described themselves may be more accurately interpreted as resistance.

The students want to be at GI, yet being there also encourages modes of behavior to which all students do not want to commit. Not all aspects of life in the fast lane are embraced. In my examples of student types (striders, defenders, socializers, and strugglers), most are clearly cases of adjustment, yet there are hints of resistance among the striders. Tracie is a kind of resister, as is Willard. I call them academic resisters, but I question whether it is resistance to the academics as much as resistance to the rush toward careers and academic specialization. They are not resisting learning.

Academic resisters question the values of their friends and the institutional values embedded in the school. Resisters espouse a philosophy that grounds their resistance. Many are among the brightest in the school, as measured by the Scholastic Aptitude Test. They are highly capable, but not motivated to spend the time or expend the effort. "I am not going to devote my life to studying," asserts one senior. These students are willing to settle for a lower grade in order to follow other interests. Some peers call them "slackers," meaning they do not spend time studying and doing the work of which they are capable. One of my strongest memories is of one strider expressing his dismay about a resisting strider peer: "Sean is one of the brightest guys here. He is a slacker. He puts off work, does not do what he can and does his own thing!"

The resisters will spend enormous amounts of time doing their own thing and then making up work they avoided. Resisters fear becoming academic drones. They see their peers as falling into three categories: academic, social, and both academic and social like themselves. They want to experience more than academics and grades, and being social is not enough either. They are interested in learning. Resisters do not value social activity over academics— they are interested in relationships. They choose to engage in activities other than studying. Their style is to do work at the last minute. They begin studying around midnight. The daytime is given to doing last-minute work and catching up on sleep. Having conversations is more important than writing. These students also recognize the limits of their behavior. When it is time, they meet the deadlines. They know how to ask for extensions. They know how to milk the system. In this next passage, I fashion an explanation of being a resister by piecing together various student comments using the voice of Milton, a senior, who thinks 30% of the school, and certainly the seniors, drive themselves in an unhealthy way.

> Those guys drive themselves toward a goal that may not be realizable. GI encourages people to do that kind of thinking. My buddies have learned how to meet our needs and roll with the pressures of the school by doing what is necessary but not going way beyond. None of us get D*. Patrick is a guy on my floor who keeps focused and will keep working until he falls asleep. He is not one of the unrealistic driven, but he never reaches the point that we do when we say that is enough, we need to do something for ourselves. We move on to sleep, to play, to talk, etc. I value comradeship, over grades and do work when it has to be done. I am willing to settle for a C and stay at GI. Others leave if they get low grades. Pursuing our own interests over simply working to get good grades is our credo. Even in courses I love I will not do the required work unless I have to do it. Life should be fuller and more meaningful than it is at GI. Our notion is there is life after GI.

The stories of pranks and resistance demonstrate that GI life has a subtlety that may not be apparent on the surface. The students find ways to express themselves within the total environment that is the Greenhouse Institute.

CURRICULUM, MEANING, AND THE VALUE OF CONTENT

My curiosity was peaked when Frank dropped by my cubbyhole office one afternoon to state as "a science person" his concern for a peer who was "a humanities person." Frank's worry was that his friend did not have more "difficult specialized courses" to take like he did in the science and math curriculum. The situation was "unfair." His humanities-loving peer should have the opportunity to be as challenged as he was as a science person.

His sincere concern for his friend's learning was heartfelt. I was startled by his use of the phrase "difficult specialized courses." I began to wonder whether other students had his inaccurate assessment of the curriculum. Was his perception a window into the values learned at the school? More than simply learning a set of facts occurs. Students learn something about the value of learning, studying, and curriculum content as well as tacit knowledge about academics. Students make choices among courses and about doing homework that reflect their understanding of the curriculum, or at least the way to make it through GI. What the curriculum at GI means to the students and what it teaches them about the value of knowledge and learning are issues that are important in a program built to be a rigorous academic program. GI has a mixed curriculum in which science, math, and humanities have comparable value. In this way the school differs from those residential high schools that specialize in a narrower range of academic talent.

In order to understand the value implicit in the curriculum, I examined what self-defined students (science person, humanities person) said. Programs like the Greenhouse Institute proudly offer content that would not exist in most ordinary high schools, and in a manner that enriches and accelerates learning. Unlike the standard high school, teachers have free reign to present content within the fuzzy limits of course descriptions. To the Teaching Fellows (recall a group of high school teachers who came to GI to learn more about teaching these students), not having a curriculum with specified scope and sequence of objectives from which they could adjust was disquieting. The custom at GI was that teachers had license to create their courses to suit their students. The freedom was similar to that of a liberal arts college. However, the freedom was really not limitless. The state curriculum requirements for an honors diploma had to be followed, as well as GI's own requirements. This still left considerable latitude for the faculty.

Teachers at GI love their content. This fact moves them to include the material they like best. The most powerful external limit on content and apparently on teaching style is the decision of some faculty to adopt the Advanced Placement notion of curriculum. In those courses, primarily in science and math, content has to be taught that matches the objectives to be tested in the exam prepared by the Educational Testing Service. Other faculty, mostly in the humanities, did not adopt the AP standard. The decisions to go either way were made by the faculty in that area. The faculties' decision was connected to a philosophy of curriculum that blends content, student beliefs, and quality standards that differentiate the divisions of science/math and humanities.

Science/Math Faculty

The science/math faculty believes that the Advanced Placement model is the best way to organize the curriculum. It provides for strong content, for assessment and placement at the front end, and for quality assurance at the conclusion of a course. The faculty prefers an external standard for setting the curriculum.

A math teacher summarized the general position of his peers on the difference between divisions.

> We give more tests, more concrete assignments, more AP courses, and in math we give them a placement test. In humanities you can fudge more easily. If a kid cannot do it, it is observable directly in our courses. That is why we are considered to have harder courses by the kids.

The AP approach is also justified as a way to save families money because students can move ahead faster through college. Even with all this rationale, there are science, math, and computer courses that are not AP courses.

The statement represents the views of the group, but does not capture the range of views among the faculty of that division. An exchange, which I paraphrase, that took place in a division-level faculty meeting about content illustrates the variance in the group. One teacher argues that the math group should teach a year of calculus that is responsive to student needs: "We should have different kinds of calculus like in many colleges." Some colleagues argue for a "main-line" kind of calculus that is taught in college math departments. They ask if it is the same content as in other calculus courses. The response was, "Who is the audience? It is not college professors; it is high school sopho-mores." The issue was unsettling to the math faculty. The counter was, "I am willing to work and stay with students as long as they need it up to the time of the exam." Helping students struggle with advanced content will benefit them in the long run. As one science teacher put it, "I prefer they struggle in a caring environment" than in the atmosphere of a university where you are simply expected "to figure it out on your own."

Teachers feel that the coursework prepares students for more advanced laboratory opportunities in college, which will accelerate their development as scientists or mathematicians. The commitment to their content area is so strong and focused that some have trouble entertaining the notion that students might have multiple interests. When I asked a math and science teacher why students might take many literature courses with heavy reading requirements, the reply was, "Bad advising."

Humanities Faculty

Humanities faculty decided to forego the Advanced Placement model for "depth and thoroughness." The faculty prefers an internal standard for determining content. However, taking an AP exam is possible. The humanities division encompasses a wide variety of disciplines, such as history, philosophy, literature, writing, and foreign languages. They represent a more diverse group of disciplines than math/science.

Humanities teachers also love their content and are concerned about quality. Among the faculty, the role of content in a course is disputed. One perspective is that the goal of a course is to get students to "go beyond obvious learning and teach them useful analytic and synthesis skills." Content is a means for setting up thinking about topics and issues, and is equal in value to thinking. A second colleague argues that thinking is more important than the content. Content is primarily important as it provides a basis for thinking. A third position is that content (facts and principles) is the most important part of the curriculum and a necessary precondition to thinking. She offers an example and question, when students are asked to write a three-page paper about the future of Russia after having read a few pages: "What is that teaching about the nature of information, facts, et cetera in an argument? Where is the context that is needed to understand what is happening?" These perspectives influence how students are taught and assessed in the humanities.

The two divisions present differing ideas of what curriculum is, and of viewing learning and knowledge. Every student takes coursework in each division. Is this associated with some courses being more valued by students than others?

Some Content Is Valued Differently

Do AP courses have higher value, maybe more status, than the non-AP courses? The answer depends on whom you ask and in what context. Students repeatedly told me that status and popularity are not issues about one's place in the social system in this school. Blocked from status as an entry to understanding the value of content, I took a different tack by asking for examples of favorite, least favorite, and challenging courses.

Challenging courses, for which students gave similar definitions, are present in each division. Challenging courses have to do with the amount of work, the quality of the teaching, and the level of thinking. But the actual value of a challenging course may rest on a fine distinction that is connected to the idea of an informal academic competition between students. (The school has no formal in-school competitions.) Competitiveness was mentioned in descriptions of conversations about grades and courses on the floors of male and female dorms. The possible connection between competition and value came out in an informal chat with two girls. Saying how well one did in a humanities course may be met with the comment, "Well, it is not the hard science courses, only literature." One girl said that this reappearing comment made her "angry" and "I yell!" Apparently, such a comment would not be made as readily about a science course. The example and Frank's question that began this section suggest that AP courses are connected to value and maybe status in the minds of some students. The AP designation and external exams are subtle influences on the student perspective. Determining which humanities class is more advanced is tricky for students because no external indicators like AP designations are available. A student must know the instructor and a little about the content to make that distinction.

On the other hand, adults who were not teachers have a clearer view. I was told that status was connected to taking Advanced Placement courses and taking math classes. I did hear more reference to high SAT scores in reference to math than to verbal or to cumulative scores, for example 1500. At the school's awards ceremony more science and math prizes are given than humanities awards. A humanities teacher who felt strongly about this difference noted that this situation is more a reflection of the number of outside groups who are willing to fund awards. In this sense the awards mirror the larger society. This point may be the key—that is, the students are products of a society that honors hard science over other "softer" disciplines. Given the context, perhaps science and math courses are more highly regarded, and the fact that they are AP course designations is a secondary consideration to their value to students.

Are there other explanations that might explain why science may become more valued by students? Science and math courses are more concrete as the term is commonly used, in other words fact-based as opposed to opinion-based. However, humanities teachers would maintain a well-structured argument based on an analysis, and understanding of the facts and context is not opinion-based, but rather is the rigor in the way Frank meant "difficult specialized courses." The term *concrete* also has a secondary meaning about the correctness of an answer. In math and science courses there is often a single right answer. In humanities courses, however, there are multiple answers, and correctness is based on the critical standard that is used. This difference is important for understanding the notion of curriculum that is operating in the minds of the students. The fact that students must take courses in both divisions with differing philosophies places them in situations where they make comments about how they view the two divisions and what the content does for them. Heavy identification with one division results in the obvious. The content and mode of teaching characteristic of that division is preferred. Yet there are many exceptions and some of these are presented in the words of the take-it-in-stride students. Note the comparative message about content.

Students State Which Content Is Valued More

George said that his science and math teachers go through a lot of content and minimize the interesting subtleties. Interesting connections are not pursued because teachers say they must cover the large amount of content for the AP exam. George's science teacher the previous year in his local high school went deeper into the topic, which helped him immensely the first semester here. George regrets not having the opportunity to get into content more deeply. "Content taught fast cannot be deep" seems to be his meaning.

Paul, a senior "science person," notes,

> The way math and science is, I guess, there's a lot of straightforward, you're fed information, you apply things from what you've learned in the past. Whereas the humanities where I have to actually produce my own opinions and present them to the class, I have difficulty just getting all my thoughts together and figuring out exactly what I want to say.

He goes on trying to explain that he is surprised that the humanities course he sort of likes is "helping me think" and helping him think in science.

Jeannie, a junior science person, says her favorite courses are in the humanities:

Yeah, it's like [laugh] I do think that [science] that's really where
my ability lies, but except the lit. classes are still so much more
enjoyable [than the science classes] because of the discussion
method. (Larry: Do you have any—this is off the topic a hair—but,
do you have any AP classes that are really sort of favorites or do they
fall in the ordinary group?) Yeah, I think those are the ordinary
because, see I really don't know if it's even possible to take AP
humanities courses. I don't know if there's any such thing.

Amelia, who is a humanities person, loves the math courses because
she thinks the way it all goes together is "kind of beautiful." As "a humanities person," she intends to be doing that kind of work in the future, but she
would not want to miss taking math courses.

Terry, who her teacher tells me in her presence has "real ability" in
science, liked the opportunity to have challenging science classes and to
see how science works. "I realize now I have an option to go into it, but I
like humanities."

Frances, who is from an impoverished background and wants to be a
physician, likes her science courses and has liked her humanities courses
much more. "You think in them," she says. The science and math courses
are "mainly memorization, not very interesting, and more of a means to an
end." That end is bypassing those courses in college. She likes problem
solving, and in her science courses the labs are the only place she can do
that.

The relationship between thinking and content as revealed by these
students is fascinating. The majority cited here opines that there is more
thinking going on in humanities courses and in the science labs than in science courses. Is there *really* less thinking in the math and science courses?
I do not know, but students think so. My hunch is that the structure of knowledge, the standards in a field, and a student's growing sense of agency interact to determine the value of content. Two different standards—external
(science) and internal (humanities)—are operating. In our world the external measure is valued. An internal personal standard does not have the same
cachet. The fields themselves are organized differently in this matter. In the
sciences a logical progression of increasingly abstract knowledge that is
supposedly universal is assumed. Predictability and an external standard
validate knowledge. In the humanities, on the other hand, knowledge is
organized around schools of critical thought and genre. Context and an
emergent internal standard determine quality. Progression requires master-
ing loosely linked schools of thought. Becoming acquainted with these tacit
organizational rules in the fields are young people who are learning the power

of their own minds and their independence. Constructing arguments in humanities courses with no external readily available standard influences students to believe that humanities courses help them think more. Yet they are paradoxically less valued.

Is it possible to answer my question about some courses being more valued by students than others? Yes. The Greenhouse Institute and our larger American culture value science more highly, but that is not the whole story.

CONCLUSION

This chapter has explored some of the complexity of the Greenhouse Institute by looking deeper into aspects of student life. Living in the fast lane involves living amidst contradiction. The meanings that students construct of the GI world are subtle as they interpret the intentions and practices of the school. The demands of academic life, especially overload, motivate students to develop strategies of dealing with homework that enable them to get it done and worry about learning it later. The tough academic load also encourages rule bending by teachers as well as counselors on behalf of students. Students learn to take advantage of that. Wellness, a program with positive intent for reducing academic stress, is seen by students as increasing the pressure. Using tests to place students in math courses points out the students' educational malnourishment. The placement forces students to make sense of their own abilities when the real issue is opportunity, not ability. The meaning and value of academic content in the school divisions of science/math and humanities raised by homework assignments and teaching practices are interpreted by students as messages or signs of difficult content. Defining oneself as a science person or as a humanities person does not mean one does not like courses in that division better than courses in the other division. Amidst the fast-paced world of GI, filled with students who came there for the academics, a resistance builds in students to academic pressure and the rush toward graduation.

CHAPTER SEVEN

A Grounded Theory
of Life in the Fast Lane

Another major part of the student experience is the social relations that form among students as they interact in this 2-year residential academic community. The Greenhouse Institute environment sets forth conditions for the participants that yield a network of social relations that is atypical when compared to local high schools. Beneath the official structure of the Greenhouse Institute lies an informal social system created by the students in this 2-year residential public high school. Students report that the social system of GI is different from their experience in their local schools. After a while, I saw the difference too: The students' social system seemed more open, inclusive, and fluid than those found in other public and private schools (Chang, 1992; Cookson & Persell, 1985; Cusick, 1973; Peshkin, 1986). This difference is significant. The existence of the GI-created system raises questions about the reasons for its creation.

SOCIAL RELATIONSHIPS

In the course of living at GI, I heard student conversations about social relationships. I prefer the broader term *social system*, in order to avoid the surplus meaning associated with friendships and to encompass all kinds of student-to-student relationships. The essence of the student view of the social system is captured by a quote from a senior, from Chapter 3, who offered a simile that the "Greenhouse Institute is like a rag quilt." She continued,

> That's what I thought GI was like because we all come from very different places and maybe we're all a little odd. You wouldn't think that if you threw us all together that we'd fit together, but like, I

> think that we do. . . . And now, we all get to explore and see what
> kinds of different groups and friends and ideas that we can have
> when we meet.

The "rag quilt" metaphor presents the student perspective of being "thrown together." Neither the administrative perspective nor parental perspectives would accept that characterization. Students in the adult view enter an environment with a specific mission and organizational structure.

Greenhouse Institute students are "thrown together" into a preexistent organization from which a network of relationships emerges. On the surface, one sees a typical urban high school. Students of different hues in varying styles of dress carry bookbags; walk to class; and converse about homework, food, and staying up late. Sticking up through the familiar pieces of the social system are students engaging in uncommon behavior. The network of relationships among students that evolves is neither fixed nor hierarchical. Groups are loosely formed with permeable, not hard, boundaries. Students move comfortably from group to group. Indicators of status and popularity are almost invisible and are minor issues of concern for students at GI. Questions about these issues often led to the response, "That does not happen here." Being different is seen, heard, and accepted. Isolated students are present, yet the circumstance is largely their choice.

As juniors become seniors, the sense of the social community remains consistent as thoughts of college entrance become dominant and nearing graduation brings feelings of estrangement, loss, and wistfulness.

The development of social relationships is central to understanding the social system. Initially new students are placed in orientation activities run by Residence Counselors and Resident Assistants. Most know no one; a few know another student from summer camps, hometown, or preview visits. Roommates are new to each other. People gravitate toward those who look and sound like them. Anxiety associated with meeting a group of strangers changes fairly quickly to feelings of relief. As one student remarks, "What's neat is that you meet strangers and they know what you are talking about [referring to home school] without having to explain it." At this point, few groups form that are reminiscent of their local high schools. Students notice after a few weeks that boundaries have not hardened and cliques have not evolved. Movement in and out of groups is relatively easy. Friends extend in all directions. Roommates are friendly, but they do not necessarily become fast friends. As one put it, "Here you are never far from a friend."

Relationships help deal with the time when classwork and homework is not going on. "You go through such crazy things here; but since you're with people who want to learn also, it makes a difference." Friends help you to keep going and live with the demands.

I think friendship's very important here because it's just so hard to get through a week. Because a week is just so sectioned off that you're like, okay, next [assignment], next one.

Relationship also causes stress. Friendships begin quickly. "You form them so fast and they're so strong; and then they can get broken really fast and just go away." Friendships are intense because one constantly encounters the same people. If a student is having a disagreement with someone else, "and everywhere I go, he's there in the dining hall, in class, in the lounge, in the computer lab. There is no time, like, I can get away and think about it." A junior student provides a view of relationship stress:

I would say that, if there's ever a person you don't, particularly like . . . it's going to be, like really bad. Because, you are going to see them a lot of the time and you have to be able to have this self-control to not act on this dislike. Because you know, when you're living in such a close environment, the relationships are going to be strained. They're either going to, be like coal turning into a diamond and being hard core; or else it's going to be crumbled to the dust and you're going to hate them.

In his view, students make choices to make their residential world livable. Girls mention lack of privacy as a factor that heightened relationship pressure. More than once, I heard, "Everyone knows what you are doing. It gets around." Among boys, being attracted to activities such as computer and role-playing games and away from studying creates stress.

The heterogeneity of friendships stands out to some students as a feature of GI life. Every student I asked reported being friendly with a person who they would not have likely been friendly with at the home school: "I have some friends that are really different and nothing like anybody I ever hung out with before."

THE COMPLEXITY OF THE SOCIAL SYSTEM

The social system appears simple, but there are subtleties in relationships and inconsistencies that helped me to better understand it. Beside the obvious forces shaping the social system, there are less visible aspects of the system that make it more complex. Not all of the 300 students know each other by name. Three factors figure into this situation: dorm arrangement, schedule, and weekends. The sexes are separated into different buildings. Choice of roommates and residence counselor is possible for seniors, but juniors have few choices. Students know others on their floor, especially in their RC group, and their classmates. Schedules are crammed and time is scarce. On weekends one third or more of the students depart for home.

Conflict

Conflict in social groups is inevitable. At GI people got annoyed, "on edge" and "pissed off." Misinterpretations of others' behavior and words happened. The constant lack of privacy in a residential school makes people edgy. The actual amount of interpersonal conflict is hard to estimate. Rarely did it happen aloud in public places. When it occurred, it happened mostly in the dorm where RCs and RAs helped smooth any incidents. Incidents about conflict might hit the student grapevine, but not with the regularity of incidents about romance. Although friction occurs, GI students report no stories of physical fights. Words are used to imply that it could happen, but it did not during the year I was there. Adults told me that physical violence had never happened in the history of the Greenhouse Institute.

Social Groups. Some collections of students are identifiable. Outsiders might identify them as cliques, but very few students do: That would be an incorrect designation in the GI community. Whenever I heard the word *clique* used by a student, I followed up at some later time to find out who constituted the clique. Students hedge their descriptions, unable to supply a picture that fit the idea of rigid boundaries implied in the term *clique*. In fact, my participants moved away from the idea. This led me to wonder if the word *clique* is used by students in a habitual way of talking about high school social systems. Students noted two groups that tended toward exclusivity: Asian Indian males and African-American females. Even though students acknowledge these groups, they do not label them as cliques. Interestingly, not all Indian males or Black females belong to those groups. In the dining hall or in the lounges, mixed groups are the standard. The boundaries are open. Even in those groupings, students of different ethnicity or sexes join the groups.

While students who are of the same or different ethnicity were accepting of some students' need to be periodically "exclusive," they seemed to chuckle that any group would really think themselves to be special. Persistent probing over the months did not produce statements about clique-like grouping having to do with race or ethnicity. It was more like the outside students felt that the members of those groups had a need that was seen as mildly different from other students in the Greenhouse Institute. I never heard any statements suggesting those groups "should change and be like us."

Diversity is a foundational notion of the school and stands out as the most compelling characteristic of the school for many students. The pervasive presence of diversity requires that they make sense of it. The students find the diversity both attractive and bewildering. The variety of ethnic and religious differences is startling, even for members of the same general ethnic group. I recall a meeting of a club of Indian students at which the members, who shared a general subcontinental culture, were not able to understand the names of foods each was describing due to the diversity of Indian culture.

The meaning of diversity at GI is multifaceted, too. Not only are racial, ethnic, and religious differences included, but urban-rural differences, gender differences, and sexual-orientation differences, as well. The first and most common meaning for diversity is racial difference, which means Black-White differences. The other races are readily apparent but are seen as tangential to the dialogue when diversity and racism are mentioned. For students, the second meaning of diversity, and a most disturbing notion for them, was sexual orientation. The presence of gay, lesbian, or bisexual classmates forces students to consider the disconnection between personal liking for someone and religious beliefs about those others. I use the word *force* because students live together 24 hours a day for 10 months. For example, statements such as, "I am a Christian and it is against my religion," are coupled with "Jim [a gay student] is a great person. I like him. He is like me."

Racism. Racism is part of the American experience since before the founding of the country. Racism exists here, too, but apparently in a GI kind of way. Interestingly, many students say it is not present; others say it is. The difference between those groups is illustrative of the atypicality of the GI social system.

Diversity was typically talked about very positively and was taken for granted. If there were strong inclinations to be negative about the topic, I did not hear them voiced. Notwithstanding, conversations about racism were experienced as discomforting by all. Blacks and Whites see the situation much differently. Both parties mention offhand comments that hint of racism. Both parties are hesitant to say that racism is actively present. All are aware that diversity is valued at GI and the environment would not support racist comments. As one student noted, "Every once in a while, there's some people who [make comments] and everybody's like, shut up now, we don't want to hear it, you shouldn't say that." Another noted, "It would not be smart," meaning racist comments do not fit in a diverse environment like the Greenhouse Institute. So-called attempts at humor is the universal descriptor of when racist comments appear.

An interesting dichotomy is how Whites and Blacks report the frequency of conversations about diversity. Whites state that diversity is a familiar conversational topic, but Blacks say it is not discussed. The split in viewpoints is due to the fact that the Black students are speaking of racism, but Whites are not. The lack of conversation about racism disturbs Black students. One student said,

> The Greenhouse Institute is such an open environment that everything gets talked about, I mean sex, drugs, everything, gets talked about except race, except race. And the thing about it, okay, if we can talk about all those things, why can't we talk about race? Is something so bad? So scary that we can't get people's opinion about the subject?

The extent to which Asian students or students from non-White ethnic groups think about racism was never clear to me. The formation of clubs linked to a specific ethnic group suggests that ethnic and racial identification is made. I am certain that they recognize their differences from others, in general, and their differences from others such as Korean or Iranian, yet those clubs have mixed membership. Some of that awareness of differences may be heightened more by being the children of immigrants with traditional culturally relevant values than by being members of the racial or ethnic group.

Dating

Dating is a small part of life at the Greenhouse Institute, and is less important than friendship. Friendships between the sexes can be seen in study sessions in the lounges and in pairs or in groups of threesomes or more leaving the dorm in the evening, in the dining hall, and in the halls of the school. Sometimes long-term friendships turn into romances, and a couple appears. These, according to the students, seem to be the couples that last. More often a romance flairs and burns out.

Sex is an ever-present topic of jokes. My sense is that there is less sexual activity at the school than in most high schools. A questionnaire answered by half the students, comprised of a relatively even proportion of males and females, indicated that dating neither occurs frequently nor occupies much time. On the weekends, there is some intense activity by a few students; and the same is true for the weekdays. Stories of sexual activity are available for listeners. I believe those stories were largely exaggerations or fabrications that are indicators of wishful interest more than activity. During a "member-checking visit" 4 months later to corroborate my findings with faculty and students, I asked for feedback. I received explanations about dating and sex that were familiar from my field notes: "We know each other so well it is like dating your sibling"; "We see so much of each other that relationships arise and end rapidly"; "We have other priorities at this time"; "This is a transition time in our lives with nothing permanent"; and "Many of us have relationships with friends outside the school."

Status and Popularity

Is there a status system at the Greenhouse Institute? Indicators of status are present in the school, although they do not seem to exert much pressure on the social relationships. Some students are concerned about their place in the school. A few adults expressed concerns about status, but rarely did students express any concern to me. I was never able to determine anything resembling a consensus about what made someone cool, popular, or attractive. I asked lots of students and the answers were always vague and inconsistent. Some terms that may be related to thoughts of status include taking challenging courses, the college you get into, being a science person and not a humanities person, and clothing. How such thoughts affect social interaction is unclear. I have limited evidence on this point. For seniors, the college to which one is admitted is a concern. At the same time, it is also an unpredictable process. Students acknowledged by peers as bright do not always get into the prestigious schools, and size of scholarships can influence a peer's (and family's) final choice. Of course, college admission becomes public in the last semester of the senior year, rather late in the life of the students at GI and in the formation of the social system. Because I concentrated my attention on juniors more than on seniors, I may have missed some changes in the system.

In sum, students at the Greenhouse Institute construct a social system that they identify as different from their home high schools and which is different from that described in the literature on high schools (Chang, 1992; Cusick, 1973). A group of diverse students from the same state who share being serious about learning enter a selective program designed to promote academic talent. A social system emerges in that high school that values diversity and excellence. In this system, differences of many kinds are accepted and appreciated, cliques do not form, boundaries among groups are permeable, movement is fluid, and academic accomplishment is valued.

HOW CAN THE SYSTEM SUSTAIN ITSELF?

Social systems are not accidental occurrences; they are constructed. The participants (students, faculty, residential counselors, and administrators) interact within the institutional context. The history of the people as well as that of the institution influences the process.

Students say repeatedly that GI is different than their local high schools. The characteristics of the GI student social system are as follows:

students see the differences among them
students accept that diversity and value difference
students see that elements reminiscent of the local school and larger
    society do not operate here
students belong to multiple groups that have permeable boundaries
when boundaries appear, students interpret their presence as inappro-
    priate, yet understandable
excellence is valued
students create a fictitious group of insiders—the GIites—representing
    the whole.

Recognizing that these descriptors are in marked contrast to how students are described in most high schools, how does the GI social system sustain itself in a world that is generally hostile to its existence? Differences based on gender, socioeconomic status, sexual orientation, race, and ethnicity exist at GI just as in American society as a whole, but the divisions are not manifested at GI. Could it be that separation from the fractiousness of our larger society is sufficient to prevent a reproduction of the larger society at GI, unlike in the typical high school? Private schools are not able to create an environment where the divisions of the larger society are not present.

What must be happening at the Greenhouse Institute that could explain what I have reported? Or is my description an artifact of my own bias, my own values, influencing what I have found? The picture I have described and these questions haunted me. I decided to use the principles of grounded theory to come to terms with this picture.

POSING ALTERNATE ASSERTIONS EXPLAINING SOCIAL LIFE

I assumed that by generating alternate assertions to explain what I observed and examining the data for support of each, I could develop an adequate explanation for how the GI social system works that is consistent with my description. Over several months I brainstormed 22 possible alternative assertions with the help of conversations with colleagues and students. The order in which they appeared is presented below.

1. Special kids come to the school
2. Special kids are from special families

3. There is a faculty and administration that promotes advanced learning, diversity, and personal responsibility
4. Stress drives the students together
5. Learners are brought together with teachers who want to teach the subject
6. Orientation to the future characterizes many students
7. The nature of the special program is transitory
8. GI has no football team, and few organized sports
9. GI displays publicly neither grades nor class ranking
10. A new basis for a social system is created
11. It's simply a nice bunch of kids
12. Socio-economic status factors are weak and the range is too narrow
13. Adults play a nurturing role and serve as models
14. Values stay similar enough for the length of the program
15. School spirit is not present in the usual sense
16. The program is a 2-year, not a 4-year program
17. Feeling different is replaced with a feeling of belonging
18. The curriculum is science, math, and humanities
19. People leave all the time
20. Students have no knowledge of other students' pasts
21. School size is small
22. School is in a residential setting

I marshaled evidence for each assertion and wrote memos to myself to that effect. For example, I wrote:

> *Assertion: GI has no football and few organized sports.* I had a chance today to talk to a boy who went to a nonresidential school that had a social system, his mother had reported and he corroborated, that sounded much like GI. When I asked what could account for that situation in his school, his immediate answer was "no football team." Does this say something about the effect of football on school environments for many students who are serious about learning? Does the football team provide a ready-made status determiner?

When writing these memos, no single assertion or combination emerged to be even partially adequate for explaining the social system. Yet some explanations merged into broader categories: kids and families, program characteristics, and disconnected (which were explanations for which I had no supporting evidence, so I eventually discounted them). In the continuing process of comparing and synthesizing the two remaining broad categories, some of the clarity and coherence of meaning disappeared. Something was missing; were my categories wrong? I began to intuit that the kids and families were external, personal factors that were brought into GI, and program characteristics were internal, structural factors that were already there. I also became aware that some assertions did not fit comfortably inside my two original broad groups yet seemed to go together. I named the new category *coalescence*. This untidy category was composed of forces that closed and opened the social system simultaneously. The tension between the forces pushed me toward a theory.

DO THE CATEGORIES EXPLAIN THE SYSTEM?

In the next section, I discuss the categories kids and families, program characteristics, and coalescence. For each category I consider the following question: Is there something about the personal category that favors an interpretation of the institutional factors that leads to this social system? The groupings are illustrated in Figure 7.1 later in the text as components of a grounded theory of social life at GI.

Kids and Families

The kids and families category is formed by the characteristics of the students and their families that are brought into the context that are likely to influence the emergence of the social system.

A selective group of children come to the Greenhouse Institute and, as such, are by definition *special kids*. Their specialness is marked in several ways: what they did to come here; who they are when they arrive; and what their families are like. Students and their families must make an effort to attend the Greenhouse Institute. They complete college-type applications, including essays, recommendations, and a portfolio, while they are sophomores. All do well on standardized measures; some have extremely high scores. All claim they are serious about learning. Many feel different and were not comfortable in their home schools, either socially, academically, or both. Some report that the local school was not encouraging of their application, so they had to persevere despite that attitude. The families have agreed to let their children leave home 2 years earlier than other college-bound children. Not all families with similarly talented children would make such a choice. In random conversations with non-GI parents who had talented children and learned of my stay at GI, they voluntarily stated how conflicted they would have been to make such a choice.

These actions suggest that the families are special. The decision of parents to sponsor their child leaving home is also indicative of the high value the family places on education and their view of their child's probable future. The families transmit values about learning, the meaning of diversity, the importance of achievement and behavior in a group. Many of the students share a vision of future activities and goals. These characteristics of kids and families are brought into the GI environment and influence the social system that emerges.

Program Characteristics

Program values that are promoted from the first day of school to graduation speeches on the last day include valuing diversity, encouraging advanced learning, and advocating personal responsibility. Faculty, residence counselors, and administrators are hired who accept the core values of GI. Adults play a nurturing role and model attitudes and behavior in the environment. In classrooms teachers acknowledge diverse ways of thinking, experiment with novel ideas, and accept original demonstrations of what one knows in subject areas. Residential Life conducts a Wellness program that mandates that students accumulate experiences that value diversity and a service program that insists that students complete hours of service devoted to the institute and to their home communities. Residence counselors play a special role by interceding in situations where conflict and intolerance appear and help students interpret their experiences. In this way, adults play the role of older peers, sometimes parent figures, helping students develop ways of dealing with the special experiences of GI. In addition, adults (residential counselors, teachers, and the admissions and career placement persons) and children form strong relationships that serve as havens of safety in the high-energy environment of GI.

Lack of information about others' behavior, past or present, is another program characteristic that influences social interaction. New students show up with nothing known about them by other students. Strangers meet. When introducing oneself to another, the student can fashion a response to become who they want to be. This first-time meeting becomes the rudimentary basis for their GI identity instead of who they were, who their brother or sister was, or who their family is. Contrary information is unlikely to appear because the school respects students' confidentiality. GI provides no information about class ranking or public display of grades.

Major sports that are associated with high prestige, such as football, are not present at GI. Thus, a ready-made basis for ascribing status is not available. Sitting in class, a student gets a sense of one's own abilities and the abilities of other students. Students freely admit that one can be outstanding in one class and somewhat average in another. Stories are swapped about how one is doing in other classes and on the SAT. One exception is that when someone wins an award from an outside source or a competition, it is announced on the e-mail system of the institute. A second exception applies to second-semester seniors. At that time a white board containing the names of the prospective graduate is displayed to which students can voluntarily indicate the name of the college to which they were accepted. A small number of students list outrageous choices, such as the Hair Academy. The result of having limited public information about a peer that could be used as status indicators means that one must deal with the individual. I have mentioned earlier several incidents where incomplete or inaccurate knowledge of a student contributed to problems in the social fabric.

The nature of the curriculum of GI is also a program characteristic that influences the shape of the social system. The curriculum is science, math, and humanities, which means that students are exposed to content they might not choose because of the variety of courses. Some find out that their self-definition is too limited, for example, "I am a humanities person," "I am a math person." New perspectives open up as the possibility of learning and thinking in novel ways becomes part of a student's experience. This open-ended kind of possibility may promote more tolerance for diversity.

Several other program characteristics may influence the functioning of the social system. Two are defining features: The program is 2 years in length and is a residential program. Both features make GI different than local high schools in obvious ways. Over the 2 years they spend at GI, students rapidly progress from novices to seniors. By the middle of the first year, they are already preparing to leave and are considering college choices. The fact that the program is residential means that the distance between home and school is eliminated. For most students this is significant because GI becomes home. One acts differently in one's home than in school. The third but nondefining feature is the withdrawal process. Children leave throughout the year for various reasons that are rarely made public. Friends, roommates, and classmates leave. For a few days that is a topic of conversation, but then it fades as the pressure of the institutional requirements inserts experiences between the fact that someone left and the immediate moment.

Coalescence

Coalescence contains alternative assertions made by me that do not fit into either the kids and family or the program characteristics categories. These assertions are close to the two categories, but do not belong with them. Rather, they are by-products of the joining of the two categories to produce a quasi-independent set of explanations. Coalescence was neither part of any person nor group nor of the institution itself. The statements comprising coalescence have a reciprocal role by pulling the system together (closing forces) and pushing the system apart (opening factors). The oppositional forces are important parts of the theory. Figure 7.1 illustrates coalescence in relation to the other categories.

Stress and *pressure* are terms often used by adults and students to describe life in the fast lane. The stress comes from the way in which the program is organized as well as from the students themselves. The persistent rapid pace of the academic and residential life program leaves students with little time to get involved in actively separating themselves from others or joining others in an exclusive group. Instead, students band together in order to deal with what is happening to them in terms of the newness of the place as juniors or to get around some of the rules.

The program does not solely generate the pressure. The students possess qualities that heighten the feeling of pressure. Seeking challenge, wanting to be the best, and desire for mastery of subject matter keep up the academic pressure. Creativity, when coupled with perfectionist tendencies and procrastination, maintains the academic pressure, too. The feeling of pressure appears to have the perverse effect of closing and opening the social system. Finding others who share their love of poetry or biology moves students closer. However, the multiplicity of interests among the student body as well as the diversity of the school population does move people apart. The presence of diversity also opens the system because students have to confront others who are different in customs, beliefs, and behavior. The resulting discomfort pushes similar kids together, as seen in the proliferation of student clubs. On the other hand, the proliferation of clubs means that students are pulled toward their multiple interests, a factor that often separates people.

The Greenhouse Institute is filled with signs of *transition*. Students know that in 2 years they will be moving on. Just as students are getting settled in as juniors, the school provides opportunities to visit colleges and meet college recruiters. A subtext for the entire senior year is college applications and acceptance. In the spring term, juniors realize that half of the students will leave in June and a new half will join them in August. They quickly move from novices to veterans. Two other practices of GI enhance the transitory feeling of the program. Students go back to their hometown and return repeatedly during the year. All leave monthly for extended weekends. Many go home on other weekends. Some go home every weekend. All see friends withdraw from GI throughout the year. Experiencing transition is so chronic, it produces a sense of *impermanence*, which is amplified by personal and familial issues that draw student attention away from GI. The students who come to GI tend to be future oriented. College is almost upon them. They are thinking of and preparing for the next step in their lives, so that many of them recognize that worries about this part of life will pass. Thoughts such as "this will

Figure 7.1. A Grounded Theory of GI Life

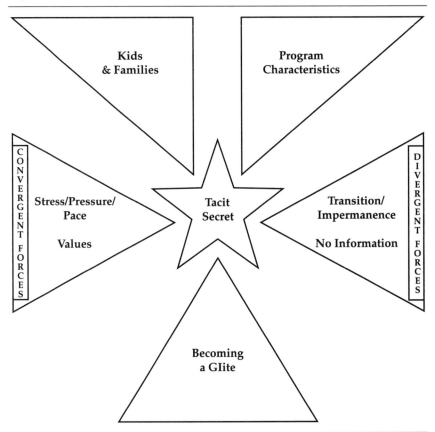

pass and I can really get on to what I want" or "this is nothing compared to how busy I will be in the future" illustrate thinking of the future. At the same time, thoughts of the future engender anxiety because of the unknown.

At the Greenhouse Institute, what is known about any individual is fragmentary and discontinuous. Because of confidentiality rules, adults generally cannot share information with students. The individual student can fashion her personal history as she sees fit. Prior school history is generally unknown. *No information* on class rank or grades is available. This lack of information keeps the social system unsettled. Finding information about someone is so difficult; it may disrupt the formation of habitual social categories. In this sense the social system is kept open. On the other hand, closeness may be promoted by getting to know each other more personally than they would in a local high school.

The Greenhouse Institute promotes coalescence by bringing together students who want to learn a subject with knowledgeable teachers who want to teach it; it is the *tacit secret* of gifted education. This description does not match most high school settings. How many times do students and teachers really *want* to be doing what is expected in the classroom? The chemistry created by the interactions between adults and students produces moments when a student knows that something worthwhile has been learned. The sense of enjoying learning amidst the pressure may enable students to transcend more mundane interpersonal issues in high schools. People who are involved in that manner may not have feelings of exclusion, or at least fewer such feelings, and are less ready to engage in exclusionary activity.

A feeling of belonging in the GI community occurs among people there. Signs of it can be heard in stories told by returning alumni when they visit; and in statements made by students about leaving for extended weekend or vacations and wanting to come back as they *become*, in their words, *GIites*, or members of the community of the Greenhouse Institute. The sense of belonging grows while at the school. The feeling of being different that the juniors bring to GI changes to a feeling of acceptance in this setting, and eventually to a feeling of belonging. Students report that they can be "more honest with others" and "be more myself" as a consequence of being at GI. The feeling of belonging supercedes or counteracts the formation of a typical system of social relationships with the chance for exclusion. Not all feel that they belong, and belonging is not a steady state. In fact, it may be the force that makes the social system appears less differentiated than in a typical high school. A second source for a feeling of belonging may be the fact that GI is a residential setting. GI does become a "home" for many students, often during their first semester there. One does not tend to exclude others in one's family. Another source of the maintenance of a feeling of belonging is that those who do not acquire that feeling withdraw from the Greenhouse Institute. They return to their home high schools to graduate. With them out of the social system, their potential to question or disrupt the feeling of belonging, which might pull apart the GI social system, is impossible.

Earlier in this text, six terms (openness, acceptance, fluidity, busyness, pressure, and shock and amazement) characterized the Greenhouse Institute. When one reflects on the discussion in Figure 7.1, these terms can be found in the three categories. The countervailing forces that open and close the system can be seen in these six terms, too. That, I believe, is the story of the Greenhouse Institute. The social system of GI is different from the regular high school because of the presence of closing and opening forces that express themselves throughout the social system. The factors in the kids and families and the program characteristics categories interact to produce the major elements, represented in Figure 7.1 as stress, values, impermanence, tacit secret, and no information to create this unusual learning community. My guess is that changing any of these elements would make the emergence of this social system unlikely.

CONCLUSION

GI is almost a *total institution*, a term coined by Goffman (1961) to describe places such as asylums, where all the elements of life are controlled. Yet unlike a total institution, GI students can decide to leave. Students have choices, although they are within a limited range set by the adults. Students participate in discussions of policy and of the enforcement of rules in some cases, but the power rests with the adults. Students resist the rules. Students do circumnavigate obstacles and negotiate rules with adults to get their needs met, but the GI is everywhere, in a metaphorical sense. When students leave for a holiday, most are ready to come back soon. When they leave the building or hang out, homework and studying in some form is waiting for them. It rests in the back of their minds most of the time that there is something more to do. That is exhausting, exhilarating, and paradoxical because they feel they belong in a place that keeps them in an unsettled state most of the time.

The Greenhouse Institute is not trying to create the precise social system that emerges, although many of GI's values are consonant with it. I believe the Greenhouse Institute creates a climate of diversity, pressure, and pace that pushes the students toward the creation of the social system that emerges in order that the students can sustain their identity as people who are serious about learning. I doubt that the Greenhouse Institute could prevent the emergence of a more typical social system unless the students were willing to exchange their experience in the home school for that of GI. I see the students tacitly agreeing, largely unknown to them at a conscious level, to ignore the forces that could divide their social relationships and to buy into the culture of the school. However, at the same time I see the school putting into operation practices that help the social system be the way it is. Thus, both parties contribute to the social system.

CHAPTER EIGHT

Metaphors and Issues in the Fast Lane

My year living in the fast lane was busy, too. Each day brought more questions and more aspects of the student experience to observe. As the process went forward, I compiled an ever-changing list of issues and concerns. In this final chapter I address some of the persistent questions I have about the Greenhouse Institute.

METAPHORS

Two metaphors have helped me understand the life of gifted students in a special program: that of a greenhouse and that of the "fast lane."

Greenhouses encourage growth by deliberate positive and negative practices. Removing weeds and pruning unhealthy branches are examples of negative practices; adjusting the fertilizer and the amount of water are examples of positive practices. Planned school practices that adjust the program to the student are the presence of counselors (clinical psychologist, academic guidance counselor, career counselors), the flexible rules for formation of student clubs, the establishment of mandatory study time, the requirements for service, the provision for individualized research projects, the evening office hours for teachers, the relative autonomy of the residence counselors, dorm programs, the community meetings of faculty and students, individual contracts, and periodic extended weekends so that students can return home. All these practices enable the school to be responsive to changes in students. Struggling students are assisted to develop appropriate study skills or personal habits for success. Students, who are unsuccessful or decide GI is not where they want to be, are helped to withdraw and return home. In this manner the Greenhouse Institute facilitates learning and shapes advanced development in the students.

"Life in the fast lane," the second metaphor, highlights the students' choice to leave their high school to cross into a rich educational context designed to further academic development. Once they enter GI, the experience of being a high school student changes dramatically. The students must attend to academics in ways they did not anticipate. Social concerns take a backseat in adolescent life. Studying and homework is persistently present. Initially, being in the company of other eager students is exhilarating and feels like the fast lane is the right place to be. Looking around, the rate of speed of other "vehicles" (students) is obvious as they come alongside, pass, or fall back. The possibility of losing control increases among the fast-moving, heavy traffic. Staying in the fast lane increases the speed; and "changing lanes" may steady the speed or decrease it, leaving the student behind. Continuing in the fast lane, the student becomes caught up in the race. The finish line ends at the end of a year and is renewed the next year with half of the drivers being new to the race.

The greenhouse metaphor coupled with the highway metaphor implies intention and being pushed forward. The source of the push appears external (the school); actually, the source is internal, too (the student). In my view, the internal push is more powerful. Students bring into the Greenhouse Institute a desire to know more, to learn more, and to achieve to a high standard. For many, their standard is idiosyncratic; for others the standard is to excel in comparison to others. No matter what the source of motivation, the students generate pressure on themselves to perform to the standard. Students reminded me repeatedly of their role as an accelerant to an already volatile situation. "It is the way we are," would be the sentiment. Once they enter the fast lane, the pace inevitably quickens. Thus, thinking that adults are pushing students oversimplifies the dynamics. At the Greenhouse Institute internal psychological forces of students meet the external educational institutional forces—that is, challenging classes, plentiful opportunities, and adult role models, to create an intense, high-energy, fast-moving achieving community that accelerates learning and development.

MISUNDERSTANDING ADVANCED DEVELOPMENT

Accepting that high school students willingly magnify pressure to perform or produce in an already pressure-filled situation is incomprehensible to many people. My own university students, most public and private school personnel I have met, and even some personnel at the Greenhouse Institute find the entire situation implausible. The likely root of nonacceptance is that the common experience of schooling for American students, which is the standard for judging normality, does not match the way GI students act. Most people have neither independently given themselves over to becoming excellent in some area, nor witnessed this in others. Pushing oneself to the point of exhaustion seems unusual, even abnormal. How could one do that? Athletics seems to be one area where that kind of overexertion is understandable; academics, much less so.

The persistent attention of GI students to academics as part of a desire to learn and excel seems unnatural, yet for these young people it is who they are. Paradoxically, accepting this internal drive is even hard for some adults (teachers and counselors) inside the Greenhouse Institute, an entire program devoted to encouraging academic talent. Single-mindedness is interpreted as a sign of being unbalanced, or a precursor for severe emotional distress, instead of an indicator of the way students can be. The place where the paradox is most evident is in the Wellness program, a residential life program.

The intriguing question is whether the goals of the Wellness program— to help students be balanced and well-rounded—makes sense within the Greenhouse Institute, which is a school intended to develop *academic* talent. The Wellness program might be appropriate for secondary students in general, but is it appropriate for this special group? Talent development, by definition, requires that a person be on the edge of his or her development and work to stay that way. It impels a person to move faster through typical age norms and to seek the most advanced ideas and skills in a field or discipline. Actually, in its most advanced form a talent transcends accepted conventions and creates new limits for the field or discipline. The motivations and standards that drive these students are, in my view, the fuel that is needed for reaching the most advanced stages in a discipline.

The Greenhouse Institute needs to redefine or recast how it pays attention to this vital aspect of talent development. For example, GI might share with students three ideas: it is understandable to have narrow advanced interests; it is normal to be advanced in development; it is natural to be uninterested in social activities. Most residence counselors, and many teachers, have limited knowledge of talent development, and few have experiences striving to develop a talent or participating in programs of this type. Those adults who have had such experiences, as well as those who told me of being heavily involved in some interest, had a more empathetic understanding of the students' experiences. They were uncomfortable with aspects of the GI program that devalued students' drive. Although I am using the Wellness program as conceived and executed as an example of the nonacceptance of uneven development, I do not mean to imply that the academic program at the school is free of this issue. Altering attitudes about advanced development are difficult to change because beliefs are learned in the context of a society that regards advanced development to be odd. The attitudes are also learned in college and graduate school, where the concept of nonuniversal development (Feldman, 1994)—the kind that applies to talents—is not addressed. I met no faculty member or counselor at GI who was familiar with the notion of nonuniversal development.

SATISFYING A THEORETICAL INTEREST ABOUT POTENTIAL TALENT AND SPECIALIZED CONTEXT

I have argued that the field of gifted and talented education should direct attention to studying people with potential talent within specialized contexts intended to develop that talent (Coleman, 1997). My contention is that ordinary interactions in special contexts are pivotal to the development of talent and are more significant for advanced development than are an individual's abilities. I believe that noncognitive behaviors manifested in those settings are momentous indicators of the power of those special contexts in furthering development. Relatively little precise information is available on these interactions. I began the study of the Greenhouse Institute as part of a general plan to obtain information on the interactions in a variety of special settings in which giftedness and talent is developed. I thought that learning more of the experience of being in such settings from the students' perspective would give me insight into the meaningfulness of ordinary interactions.

I believe that what I uncovered justifies my theoretical approach and my methods, but that is not the full story. I missed much of what I wanted to learn. Once at the Greenhouse Institute, I was swept up in the fullness of life and was unable to get to as close to specific interactions as I would have liked. In conceiving studies of potential talent meeting a special setting, I did not appreciate the complexity of what I was seeking and the amount of resources needed to do it. As a lone researcher, getting to specific patterns of interaction was beyond my reach in such an expansive setting as this special residential high school. I needed to devote more time in the whole school setting in order to understand the context of the narrower, more contained contexts, such as a class, a club, a lab, a floor of the dorm. I ran out of time: I simply could not be a participant observer long enough to uncover more than general patterns. Looking deeper was too fragmentary to make statements like I had anticipated finding. A team of researchers is needed over a longer period of time to study smaller interactions.

Although I did not get to the level of observation I wanted, I learned much about being a student at the Greenhouse Institute. General patterns were revealed, such as studying and doing homework as well as the discovery of institutional factors and forces operating to produce the open-ended social community. In addition, some perplexing patterns were revealed, such as the academic resistance; misunderstanding about advanced development; the value of knowledge, discussed in the last chapter; and adapting to stress that may be maladaptive. These findings raise interesting issues that I would like to comment on more directly than I have up to this point.

LOOKING CLOSER AT ISSUES

The importance of institutional characteristics cannot be overstated. The Greenhouse Institute has primary characteristics that make it much different than typical high schools. These institutional characteristics are: a 2-year program, no public grading, no major sports teams, students who choose to be there, teachers who teach what they love, and the fact that the school is residential. The confluence of this particular set of primary characteristics induces the creation of a social system that honors diversity and excellence. I have mused about the relative influence and contribution of each characteristic to the system and have found no way to quantify the relationships. I am certain that removal of any of these would change the dynamics of the system, but how much the system will change is unknown.

I also suspect that the primary characteristics combine to yield secondary characteristics that are quite influential. One is the lack of readily available status markers on which judgments can be made about other students. Another is that GI is not specialized enough to develop a single talent; rather, it develops broad, academic talent. In this way there is no real end to what is learned and developed; just a new beginning.

The combination of residential and academic components seems to produce the "who-owns-the-kids" phenomenon. Essentially, each group— RCs and teachers—claim to have the best interest of the students in mind and believes the other group does not really appreciate their contribution to the program. I saw this issue in my first months at GI as a pernicious issue. Now I have a different opinion. When I have presented papers where I have described the claims of ownership from teachers and counselors at GI without stating my negative opinion, some members of the audience have volunteered that my description sounded familiarly like what they hear in their own combined programs. Is this a universal characteristic of such combined programs? It may be. I think the sentiment that our group (RAs or teachers) alone has the best interests of the students at heart (ownership) is produced by people who are committed to what they are doing, value it over other actions in the setting, have little time or interest in learning what the other is doing, and feel overworked and underappreciated. I see the pride and paranoia in the statement of ownership as an adaptive mechanism of adults to deal with the intensity of such an intense environment.

Is it desirable to eliminate the ownership phenomenon? Some of the friction seems unnecessary. Yet the grounded theory I have induced indicates that contradictions are irritants that keep the community system fluid, keep ideas flowing, and help GI to be the special place that it is. I believe open conversations on this topic would be sufficient to keep this phenomenon in check.

How stressful is the GI environment? Stress is in the eye of the beholder. Students in similar situations do not experience stress in the same way. Furthermore, the students and the school cocreate stress. It appears that stress is a natural part of this setting. Must the Greenhouse Institute be such a stressful environment? Tolerating and adapting to stressors is a part of life in the fast lane. Survival means adapting quickly. GI attempted to reduce stress by teaching personal management and study skills. I was told that this was offered repeatedly in the school's history, but students did not take advantage of the opportunities. During my year at GI, efforts did not work. Students would justify not participating by saying they were too busy to do it. I suspect that if they had the time, many students would devalue the GI program because of their increased free time! A study I conducted in another context leads me to this conclusion (Coleman & Cross, 1993). Even so, GI should continue to work on ways to help students find healthy ways to deal with stress.

Students adapt to the school's stress and successfully complete the GI curriculum and requirements. However, some coping strategies that make sense in the immediate GI environment might inhibit later development and teach behavior that is contradictory to the mission of the Greenhouse Institute. Two adaptive academic behaviors that might have such implications are completing assignment by faking having done it; or after procrastinating, complaining about overload to get a deadline extended. These examples are minor, but if such patterns of manipulation are overlearned and become habits, then they subvert the primary goals of the school—maintaining a love of learning and pursuing knowledge for its own sake. A longitudinal study would have to be conducted in order to determine the credibility of this point.

My discovery that students develop resistance to the academics was startling. After all, the students purposefully chose to be at the Greenhouse Institute. How could they be fighting against GI doing what it promised to do? I see academic resistance as a coping strategy to the rush forward. Resistance is not indicative of distress. Academic resisters are neither educationally malnourished nor have lower ability. In fact, some of the brightest students, as measured by tests, are resisters. The proportion of resisters seems slightly higher for self-defined humanities people than for science and math people. Peers viewed academic resisters as slackers who were capable of handling the load. Basically, resisters fight to keep a perspective on their future development. In Chapter 6 I implied that the resisters seemed to continue to embrace the adolescent peer culture that they value, and to fight the rush to focus on a career path. They want to keep their alternatives open, but both GI and larger culture is telling them it is time to be serious about their future and to choose a career. They want to keep their alternatives open, but both the school and the larger culture is telling them to get serious about their futures. Nonresister peers cannot understand why they do it and the resisters cannot understand why they drive themselves in ways that limit the social and academic opportunities. I had a feeling as I listened to explanations that under the surface, both resisters and nonresisters have a grudging respect for each other.

Academic resistance may not be without its consequences. I have no data to support my theory, but I suspect that the development of academic talent slows down in resisters as they figure out where they are going and what they want to do. In that sense, they are less likely to be early stars in the fields they eventually choose. The way in which their interests and attitudes will change in the future is of interest to me. I wonder when they will settle into a role in life.

UNEXPLORED STORIES AND QUESTIONS

The story that I have told is only one of many possible stories of the Greenhouse Institute. I liken my work as an ethnographer to that of a sculptor looking at a piece of marble or wood, seeing something in that piece, slowly working the surface to remove material to reveal the hidden beauty, finding something else of beauty on the way, and anxiously deciding what to complete. A different artist might see another image in the same stone, and create a different work. As I have read and reread my field notes and interviews, I realize how much of the GI life I left behind by pursuing the story I have told.

The influence of socioeconomic status on students' experiences is an untold story. I have incomplete information on this topic. Students from varying socioeconomic statuses come to the school. The school tries to reduce concerns that the school may be unaffordable by providing assistance to some students such as paying for their books, giving them opportunities to earn money, and so on. Two student informants worked in jobs outside GI while in school.

Lack of money can have an obvious and subtle effect. The use of free time is connected to money. Trips and "runs" to movies and malls require money, as does leaving campus to eat in the strip of restaurants near the campus. Another place where resources might be apparent is the amount of technology in the dorm rooms. However, the variations of which I was aware seemed to be more connected to gender rather than income. In any case, GI has enough computers for use by any student, and students seem to share videogames and visit each other's rooms. The one place in which economic circumstances show up clearly is on the weekends and during the May term, when there are overseas travel opportunities. On weekends, the situation is complicated by distance. Students who live hundreds of miles away cannot readily go home because of time, not only because of the cost of transportation.

The female experience of GI is another story that is somewhat incomplete. My prime informants were four men and four women. I did try to keep my secondary informants—people I talked with but did not record— in roughly equal proportions of men and women. But being a male and living in the boys' dorm handicapped me, in a sense. I had less opportunity for casual contacts in the act of daily living with women. I formed a focus group of females and talked with minority females as much as possible to make up for this lack. Even so, I never felt as connected to their experiences as I did to the males' experience. Although I tried to stay cognizant of gender-related issues, I am less confident of how my general statements about life in the fast lane apply to young women.

In the GI community there are other stories that were left unexplored. I list some of them below as a suggestion of areas others might want to explore at GI or similar institutions.

The effect of leaving GI when a student goes home
Living on the girls' side of the dorm
The reclusive or very quiet students
Development of individuals over 2 years
More specific study of specialized teacher-student interactions

CHANGING MY UNDERSTANDING OF TALENT DEVELOPMENT

The study of the life of students in the Greenhouse Institute has changed my thinking about talent development in education. Some thoughts are clarifications; other thoughts are grounds for further speculation about such schools.

At GI I found a strong example of excellence and diversity being honored by students and faculty. Students and faculty concur on the importance of each concept and apparently act on it. Diversity is often used as a code word for equity in present-day America, and I think it applies in this circumstance, too. In my experience, statements often answer calls for diversity by asserting that striving for excellence will be lost. This is certainly not the case here. The GI story is not free from friction between excellence and diversity, even with the general positive regard for these values. The administration and the student body keep these ideas current in the life of the institution, as evidenced by discussions in public meetings between students and administration and in meetings of only students or only adults. I interpret the situation to mean that honoring excellence and diversity requires active attention.

The Greenhouse Institute is a special setting that cannot escape its genesis. GI mirrors the American society that created it, yet it does not recreate all of what is there. For example, signs of racism and anti-intellectualism are present, but play a minor role, as shown throughout this book. Materialism—the desire for goods and money in their future—is a strong pull for these students. Responses to questions about why students do an activity or where they hope to be in the future were usually filled with reference to success and material gain, such as "I wat to be like Bill Gates." Many students, particularly the goal-directed students discussed in Chapter 3, want a long-term career that garnered wealth and recognition. I recall few students talking about a career that was attractive because of the work itself or for the career's intrinsic worth, such as minister, professor of Old English, or teacher.

GI sensitized me to the pernicious effect of being educationally malnourished. Seeing talented teenagers with hurt expressions and doubting their own ability was disturbing. Even when students have enough talent to get into a school like GI, they still enter a half step behind, because of limited educational offering in their former schools. Following from the principle that teachers should teach adolescents at their own ability levels, then educationally malnourished children should start at a different place. Ironically, the students interpret their placement as a lack of ability rather than a sign of their lack of experience and educational opportunity in their hometown. The larger question is, How can the Greenhouse Institute help talented and educationally malnourished children make sense of this difference? Providing rich educational opportunity is crucial, but it does not deal directly with this deeper issue of self-worth. In the rapidly moving, information-packed courses at GI, making up the ground for what you never learned is very difficult when you cannot catch your breath because of all that is happening. I saw instances where individual students working one-on-one with teachers made up this ground. I marvel at both commitments. GI might be able to turn this situation around by providing for "catching-up" summer classes before entrance, and giving attention to the issue in counseling situations.

I appreciate the inner drive of children more than ever and its connection to specialized educational settings devoted to developing talents. Students who do not have that inner motivation to pursue a talent are unlikely to thrive in a setting that is designed to nourish that talent. This seems like a tautology, but it is more than that. The tacit secret of talent development is the joining of fast, eager learners in an area or discipline with teachers who love their content. The result is magic in the form of challenging classes, teachers with high expectations for themselves and students, and students willing to go the extra mile to learn and do something. I would like to understand the magic so that it might be recreated in other, similar, settings.

However, the Greenhouse Institute is not for everyone. GI is an inappropriate educational placement for most teenagers. The most obvious are those with insufficient potential for academic talent and no inclination to leave home 2 years earlier than most students their age. Another obvious indicator is that many of those who enter find in the first semester that GI is not for them and withdraw. Most leave during or after one semester. *Withdrawal*, the GI term for leaving, happens throughout the year.

A straightforward explanation is that students find that GI is the wrong place for them. The general reason is that GI was unable to substitute someone or something that they miss from their home environment. Examples are girlfriends and boyfriends, family ties, one's own room, an athletic team, lenient rules, or time free from constant future assignments and deadlines.

I believe that widening the net to include more students would destroy GI and what the school has been able to create with young talented adolescents. I recognize the dilemma it creates for our society, where we apparently have limited resources for education. In modern America most resources for developing talent go to athletic talents, in contrast with academic talent. Are we promoting the talents we value the most?

I think the Greenhouse Institute is successful in bringing the right people together to bring into being a powerful program that advances the learning and development of the students. GI acts on the edge of students' development, and I see the school's program as living on the edge of a precipice as well. There are potential dangers at GI, which may be a danger for any schools of this type. One danger is that the students have to contend with their talent and their own limits. Not everyone can be the best, the most advanced. The school has to be sensitive to adolescents learning how to live with this knowledge. The school seems to do a good job with this.

A second set of dangers is comprised of dangers that are not operational now, but I have a sense that they could be. Right now, GI develops talent, encourages applications to college and universities, and keeps its students connected to the community through service learning. If in the future, admittance to prestigious schools of higher education becomes the standard for being successful, then the curriculum and relationships would be adjusted and a new set of pressures would emerge that might tip the balance that fosters excellence and diversity. Another future danger is the "institutionalization" of the faculty, counselors, and administration. GI is an attractive place to work. The faculty has the luxury of offering courses with more freedom than most high school teachers and less demand for scholarly productivity than most college faculties. GI has its stresses, but it does not have the administrative and crowd control issues of local high schools. These attractive features keep people in their positions. That is positive because it adds stability to the culture, and it is negative because experience leads to valuing the past too much. If GI becomes focused on the past ways, the program will have trouble renewing itself and being responsive to changes in students and in fields of knowledge. The Greenhouse Institute must guard against parochialism. The faculty may need time for reinvigorating its knowledge and time for reconnecting with the world of adolescence and typical high schools.

CHANGING MY UNDERSTANDING OF RESEARCH

This study confirms my initial belief that ethnography is an exercise in dealing with limitations of method, thought, creativity, and narrative. The story of "life in the fast lane" looks like a straight line from conception to execution to interpretation, but that is an artifact of writing research. The fuzziness of constructs, the incompleteness of conception, and the vagaries of living maintain the gap between intention and actuality. My basic fieldwork strategy was to "go with the flow." Most decisions were an amalgamation of hunches, compromises, and luck. I thought about what I was trying to learn, developed a plan, and tried to be responsive to the study's purpose.

I struggled with alternate or rival explanations for what I witnessed. I could not know how my subjectivity was influencing the project. Too many chunks of data associated with changing contexts over time made it complex. I learned the importance of prolonged engagement and multiple sources as a check.

My faith in planning, as well as my belief in hanging loose, were reinforced. Serendipity is a mysterious part of the process. I now believe that purposeful serendipity is a research strategy. Profiting from the unexpected seems connected to maintaining a "beginner's mind." I have come to appreciate the power of purposeful sampling in collecting information from varying perspectives. Let the story emerge from the sources; the story is there.

My plans and my musings outstripped what I could do in real time. I begrudgingly learned to accept my own limitations a little more easily. Fighting to meet an undefined standard of "enough" and "thoroughness" is my typical style. In that sense, I was my own enemy.

Doing ethnography interferes with a normal personal life. Being a stranger and being alone were constants in this field. Both distort relationships. Both suggest physical distance from people, but emotional distance was my issue. Being a stranger in the field alters friendship and communication. Every contact has the potential for providing information. Participants were wary and should have been. Sometimes wariness moved toward friendship. That was evident when personal issues surfaced that one would not share with a stranger. If I was no longer a stranger, was I a friend? What kind of friend systematically makes a record for future analysis?

Being alone and away from home twists family relationships, too. The sharing of feelings with loved ones on a daily basis was missing. The distance made the sharing difficult and intensified the feeling of being alone. I found maintaining intimacy repressed by the need for maintaining confidentiality of my participants. Carefully editing what I say is not a regular part of my life. I was never at ease with this part of the process with friends or family.

LAST WORDS

All societies encourage talent, indirectly and directly, through the pervasive, subtle expression of values and the deliberate building of institutions. GI is one such institution. Can the GI I experienced be replicated? Not exactly: the conditions and people who created the place where I lived were in that moment not future moments. Under similar conditions, the GI I have described might be approximated. I have visited GI several times since I left and I see echoes of my year. At the same time, I doubt the GI community system is singular. Similar programs might be created with different students, curricula, faculty, and resources.

The story of life in the fast lane at the Greenhouse Institute is surely my interpretation of a complex local environment. I believe I have found something of the universal, as Sartre might say, in similar settings in Western culture. I hope this study encourages others to study people who are gifted in specialized settings where advanced development is intended. I believe those settings are where we will move closer to understanding how people choose to strive toward the limits of their capacity and, maybe, learn more about our own humanity.

References

Bloom, B. S. (1985). *Developing talent in young people.* New York: Ballantine.

Chang, H. (1992). *Adolescent life and ethos: An ethnography of a US high school.* London: Falmer Press.

Coleman, L. J. (1995). The power of specialized environments in the development of giftedness: The need for research on social context. *Gifted Child Quarterly, 39,* 171–176.

Coleman, L. J. (1997). Studying ordinary events in a field devoted to the extraordinary. *Peabody Journal of Education, 72*(3 & 4), 117–132.

Coleman, L. J., & Cross, T. C. (1988). Is being gifted a social handicap? *Journal for the Education of the Gifted, 11,* 41–56.

Coleman, L. J., & Cross, T. C. (1993). Relationships between programming practices and outcomes in a summer residential school for gifted adolescents. *Journal for the Education of the Gifted, 16,* 420–441.

Coleman, L. J., & Cross, T. C. (2001). *Being gifted in schools: Issues of development, guidance and teaching.* Waco, TX: Prufrock.

Cookson, P., & Persell, C. (1985). *Preparing for power: America's elite boarding schools.* New York: Basic Books.

Cusick, P. A. (1973). *Inside high school: The student's world.* New York: Holt, Rhinehart & Winston.

Denzin, N., & Lincoln, Y. (1994). (Eds.). *Handbook of qualitative research.* Thousand Oaks, CA: Sage Publications.

Feldman, D. (1994). *Beyond universals in cognitive development* (2nd ed.). Norwood, NJ: Ablex.

Glazer, B., & Strauss, A. (1967). *The discovery of grounded theory: Strategies for qualitative research.* New York: Aldine de Gruyter.

Goffman, E. (1961). *Asylums: Essays on the social situation of mental patients and other inmates.* Garden City, NY: Anchor.

Greenhouse Institute. (1996). *The Greenhouse Institute student handbook.*

Peshkin, A. (1986). *God's choice: The total world of a Fundamentalist Christian school.* Chicago: University of Chicago Press.

Strauss, A., & Corbin, J. (1990). *Basics of qualitative research: Grounded theory procedures and techniques.* Newbury Park, CA: Sage Publications.

Vygotsky, L. (1978). *Mind in society: The development of higher psychological processes* (M. Cole, V. John-Steiner, S. Scribner, & E. Souberman, trans.). Cambridge, MA: Harvard University Press.

Vygotsky, L. (1987). *The collected works of L. S. Vygotsky.* New York: Plenum.

Index

About the Author

I am a teacher who became a professor. Both enable me to be a perpetual student. In the course of my professional career I have been a student, a counselor, a teacher of children with varying special education labels, a professor of special education, a developer of programs, an advocate, an editor, a researcher, and an administrator. I have been most fortunate to have grown up in a time when I could do things that I value.

The professional activities of which I am most proud are: creating, with colleagues from three different fields, an innovative teacher preparation program based on the model of teaching as a talent; building the Summer Institute for Gifted Children in 1980, which has been "taken over" by the original students who attended it; writing a few papers that have been accepted by colleagues as new contributions to my field; and continuing to be excited by my work. My scholarly interests are the experience of being gifted, talent development in context, teacher thinking, action research/practical inquiry, and theoretical analysis.

In the 2001 academic year, I moved from the University of Tennessee (after many years) to the University of Toledo to start an innovative program to prepare teachers of the gifted. At present I serve as editor of *Journal for the Education of the Gifted*. My latest book with Tracy Cross, *Being Gifted in Schools*, is going into its second edition. Awards I have received are a Fulbright study grant to India, the 2000 Distinguished Scholar Award of the National Association for Gifted Children, and 2001 Best Paper of the Year for *Gifted Child Quarterly*.